Why knowledge of 88 the most popular Excel formulas is so important? 4

Why knowledge of 88 the most popular Excel formulas is so important?

Knowledge of the 88 most popular Excel formulas is crucial for several reasons, especially for individuals working in data analysis, finance, business, and various other fields. Here are some key reasons why this knowledge is important:

- **Efficiency and productivity:** Knowing popular Excel formulas helps users perform tasks more efficiently. Formulas automate calculations, saving time and reducing errors compared to manual calculations.
- **Data analysis:** Excel formulas are essential for data analysis. Functions like SUM, AVERAGE, COUNT, and others enable users to quickly analyze and summarize large datasets.
- **Decision-making:** Effective use of formulas allows for better decision-making. Users can create dynamic reports and dashboards, enabling stakeholders to make informed decisions based on accurate and up-to-date information.
- **Financial modeling**: In finance and accounting, Excel formulas are critical for financial modeling, budgeting, forecasting, and various financial analyses. Formulas such as NPV, IRR, and financial functions are commonly used in these scenarios.
- **Business intelligence:** Excel is often used as a tool for business intelligence. Knowledge of formulas allows users to transform raw data into meaningful insights, aiding strategic planning and business decision-making.
- **Automation:** Excel formulas are the foundation for automation. By linking cells and creating dynamic formulas, users can build automated systems that update and recalculate data as inputs change.
- **Cross-Industry Applicability:** Excel is widely used across different industries and professions. Knowing the most popular formulas provides a universal skill set that is applicable in various job roles.
- **Collaboration and communication:** Excel is a common platform for collaboration and communication. Understanding popular formulas

ensures effective communication and collaboration with colleagues, especially when sharing and interpreting spreadsheets.

- **Career advancement:** Proficiency in Excel, including knowledge of popu ar formulas, is often a sought-after skill in the job market. It can enhance career opportunities and open doors to roles that require data analysis and spreadsheet management.
- **Problem-solving:** Excel formulas empower users to solve complex problems by providing a flexible and powerful toolset. Whether it's statistical analysis, scenario planning, or data manipulation, knowing the right formulas is key to effective problem-solving.

In summary, the knowledge of the 88 most popular Excel formulas is a valuable skill set that can enhance efficiency, support data-driven decision-making, and contribute to professional success in a variety of fields.

ABS

The ABS formula in Excel is used to return the **absolute value of a number**. The absolute value is the distance of a number from zero without considering its direction (positive or negative). Here's a practical example:

Let's say you have a column of numbers representing the differences between budgeted and actual expenses in cells B1 through B5:

If you want to find the absolute differences, you can use the ABS formula. Here's how you would do it:

1. Select the cell where you want the absolute difference to appear. Let's say you want the result in column C, starting from **C1**.
2. Type the following formula in cell C1: **=ABS(B1)**.

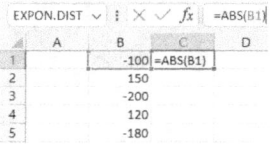

3. Drag the fill handle (a small square at the bottom-right corner of the cell) down to apply the formula to the entire column.

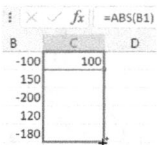

Excel will calculate the absolute value for each number in column B and display the results in column C. The formula **=ABS(B1)** returns the absolute value of the number in cell B1.

The results in column C will be:

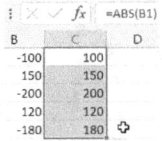

So, the practical application here is using the ABS formula to find the absolute values of numbers, which can be useful when you want to focus on the magnitudes of differences or distances without considering the direction (positive or negative).

AND

The AND formula (logical product) in Excel is a logical formula that returns TRUE if all its arguments are true; otherwise, it returns FALSE. It's often used in conjunction with other formulas to perform conditional tests. Here's a practical example:

Let's say you have a worksheet that tracks student grades, and you want to determine if a student has passed a course based on two conditions:

1. The student's score in the exam (in cell B1) should be greater than or equal to 70.
2. The student should have attended at least 80% of the classes (in cell C1).

Here's how you could use the AND formula to check both conditions:

Assuming that

- Cell B1 contains the exam score.
- Cell C1 contains the attendance percentage.

In cell D1, you can use the following formula:

`=AND(B1 >= 70, C1 >= 80)`

This formula checks if both conditions are met:

- **B1 >= 70**: Checks if the exam score is greater than or equal to 70.
- **C1 >= 80**: Checks if the attendance percentage is greater than or equal to 80.

If both conditions are true, the AND formula returns TRUE. If any of the conditions is false, it returns FALSE.

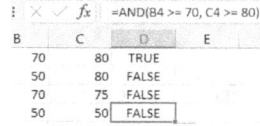

You can then use the result of the AND formula in your worksheet or combine it with other logical formulas to further analyze or display information based on the conditions.

For example, you might use an IF statement to display "Pass" or "Fail" based on the result:

`=IF(AND(B1 >= 70, C1 >= 80), "Pass", "Fail")`

This formula will display "Pass" if both conditions are true and "Fail" otherwise.

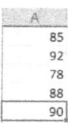

AVERAGE

The AVERAGE formula in Excel is used to calculate the **arithmetic mean of a range of numbers**. Here's a practical example:

Suppose you have a column of quiz scores for a class of students in cells A1 through A5:

A
85
92
78
88
90

To find the average score, you can use the AVERAGE formula. Here's how you would do it:

1. Select the cell where you want the average to appear. Let's say you want the result in cell **B1**.
2. Type the following formula: **=AVERAGE(A1:A5)**
3. Press **Enter**.

Excel will calculate the average of the numbers in the range A1 to A5 and display the result in the selected cell (B1 in this case). The formula **=AVERAGE(A1:A5)** calculates the sum of the numbers in the specified range and divides that sum by the count of numbers in the range.

The result in cell B1 will be: 86.6.

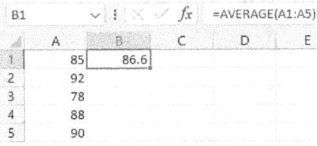

So, the practical application here is using the AVERAGE formula to quickly find the average score without manually adding up each individual score and dividing by the number of scores. This is particularly useful when dealing with large datasets.

AVERAGEIF

The AVERAGEIF formula in Excel is used to calculate the **average of a range of cells based on a specified condition**. Here's a practical example:

Suppose you have a worksheet that contains the scores of students on different quizzes. The scores are in column A, and the corresponding student names are in column B. You want to calculate the average score for a specific student, let's say "John."

Your data might look like this:

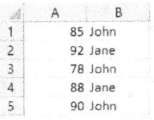

To find the average score for John, you can use the AVERAGEIF formula. Here's how you would do it:

1. Select the cell where you want the average to appear. Let's say you want the result in cell **C1**.
2. Type the following formula: **=AVERAGEIF(B1:B5, "John", A1:A5)**
3. Press **Enter**.

This formula calculates the average of scores in column A where the corresponding name in column B is "John." The syntax is **AVERAGEIF(range, criteria, average_range)**, where:

- **range**: The range of cells to be evaluated based on the specified criteria (in this case, the names in column B).
- **criteria**: The condition that determines which cells to include in the average (in this case, "John").
- **average_range**: The range containing the values to be averaged (in this case, the scores in column A).

The result in cell C1 will be the average score for John:

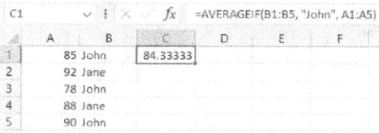

So, the practical application here is using the AVERAGEIF formula to calculate the average score for a specific condition, in this case, the scores associated with a particular student.

AVERAGEIFS

The AVERAGEIFS formula in Excel is an extension of the AVERAGEIF formula and allows you to calculate the average based on multiple criteria. Here's a practical example:

Suppose you have a worksheet that contains the scores of students on different quizzes. The scores are in column A, the corresponding student names are in column B, and the class levels are in column C. You want to calculate the average score for a specific class level, let's say "Class A."

Your data might look like this:

	A	B	C
1	85	John	Class A
2	92	Jane	Class B
3	78	John	Class A
4	88	Jane	Class B
5	90	John	Class A

To find the average score for "Class A," you can use the AVERAGEIFS formula. Here's how you would do it:

1. Select the cell where you want the average to appear. Let's say you want the result in cell **D1**.
2. Type the following formula: **=AVERAGEIFS(A1:A5, C1:C5, "Class A")**
3. Press **Enter**.

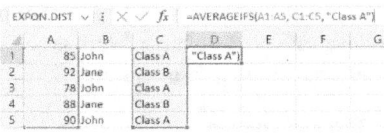

This formula calculates the average of scores in column A based on the condition that the corresponding class level in column C is "Class A." The syntax is **AVERAGEIFS(average_range, criteria_range1, criteria1, criteria_range2, criteria2, ...)**, where:

*   **average_range**: The range containing the values to be averaged (in this case, the scores in column A).
*   **criteria_range1**: The first range of cells to be evaluated based on the specified criteria (in this case, the class levels in column C).
*   **criteria1**: The condition that determines which cells to include in the average (in this case, "Class A").

The result in cell D1 will be the average score for "Class A":

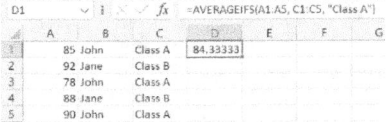

So, the practical application here is using the AVERAGEIFS formula to calculate the average score based on multiple criteria, such as the class level in this example.

CELL

Let's consider a scenario where you want to create a summary report that includes information about specific cells, such as their **addresses, values, and formatting**. The `CELL` formula can be helpful in retrieving this information.

Assume you have data in cells A1 to A5 as follows:

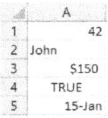

Now, you want to create a summary in cells B1 to B5 that provides information about the corresponding cells in column A. Here's how you might use the `CELL` formula for different types of information:

Get the Cell Address (Row and Column):

In cell B1, you can use the following formula to get the address of the cell in A1:**=CELL("address", A1)**

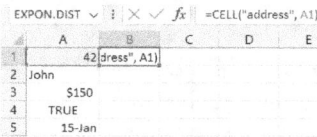

The result in B1 will be:**A1**

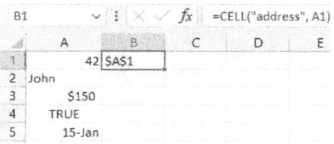

Get the value of the cell:

In cell B2, use the formula **=CELL("address", A1)** to get the value of the cell in A2:

The result in B2 will be:

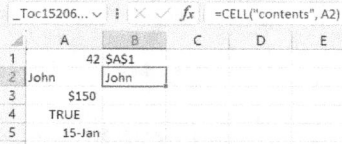

Get the formatting of the cell:

In cell B3, use the formula to get the formatting of the cell in A3: **=CELL("format", A3)**

The result in B3 will depend on the formatting applied to the cell.

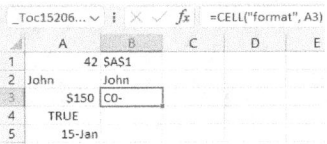

The code representing the formatting returned by the **CELL("format", ...)** formula in Excel can be a combination of letters and numbers, and its interpretation may not be straightforward. The code can vary based on the complexity of the formatting applied to the cell. Here are a few examples:

- **General format**: If the cell has a general format, the code might be "G."
- **Number format**: If the cell has a number format, the code might include letters and numbers to represent the format. For example, "C0" represents a currency format with zero decimal places.
- **Text format**: If the cell has a text format, the code might be "T."
- **Date format**: Date formats might include letters like "yy" for the year or "m" for the month. For example, "mm/dd/yyyy" represents a date format with the month, day, and year.
- **Font formatting**: Font formatting information can be represented by a combination of letters and numbers. For example, "B3" might indicate bold text, and "U2" might indicate underlined text.

Similar situation is in cells A4 and B4.

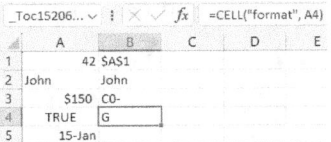

It's important to note that the interpretation of these codes can be complex, and they depend on the specific formatting applied to the cell. Also, the CELL formula may not cover all formatting details, and some information may not be directly access ble through this formula.

Get the type of data in the cell:

In cell B5, use the formula to get the type of data in the cell in A5: **=CELL("type", A5)**

The result in B5 will be:

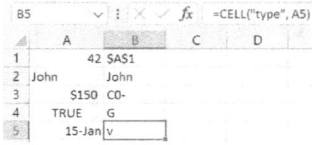

Here are some of the common types of information that the CELL formula can return:

- **address**: Returns the address of the cell as text. For example, =CELL("address", A1) might return "A1," indicating that the cell is located in column A, row 1.
- **contents**: Returns the value of the cell. For example, =CELL("contents", A1) might return the content of cell A1, such as a number, text, or date.
- **format**: Returns the formatting of the cell. This can include information about font color, bold/italic/underline settings, and more. The result might be a code representing the formatting.
- **type**: Returns a code indicating the type of data in the cell. For example, "l" represents text, "v" represents a value (number or date), "b" represents a formula, and so on.
- **color**: Returns the color of the cell's font. This can be useful for conditional formatting. The result is a number representing the color index.
- **filename**: Returns the full path and filename of the workbook.
- **prefix**: Returns a single quotation mark (') if the cell contains left-aligned text.

These are just examples, and the actual results will depend on the specific content and formatting of the cells in column A. The `CELL` formula can be a powerful tool for creating dynamic summaries or reports that provide detailed information about cells in your Excel workbook.

CHOOSE

The CHOOSE formula in Excel is used to select and return a **value from a list of values based on a given index number**. Here's a practical example:

Suppose you have a sales dataset with various products, and you want to calculate the commission rate for each product category. You have a commission rate table in cells F1:G4, where column F contains the product categories, and column G contains the corresponding commission rates:

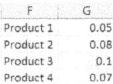

F	G
Product 1	0.05
Product 2	0.08
Product 3	0.1
Product 4	0.07

Now, in your main dataset in column A, you have a list of products:

	A
1	Product 3
2	Product 1
3	Product 2
4	Product 4

You want to calculate the commission rate for each product based on the commission rate table. You can use the `CHOOSE` formula for this purpose.

In cell B1, you can use the following formula:

=CHOOSE(MATCH(A1, F1:F4, 0), G1, G2, G3, G4)

Here's a breakdown of the formula:

- **MATCH(A1, F1:F4, 0)**: Finds the position of the product in cell A1 with n the product categories in column F. The third argument, 0, indicates an exact match.
- **CHOOSE(MATCH(...), G1, G2, G3, G4)**: Uses the `MATCH` result as the index to choose the corresponding commission rate from the list of values in cells G1 through G4.

So, if A1 contains "Product 3," the formula would return the commission rate for Product 3 from cell G3 (0.10). If A2 contains "Product 1," it would return the commission rate for Product 1 from cell G1 (0.05), and so on.

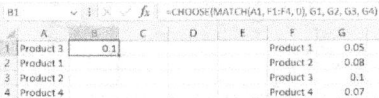

You can then copy this formula down for the other cells in column B to calculate the commission rates for the entire product list.

This is a simplified example, and in a real-world scenario, you might have a larger dataset with more products and commission rates. The `CHOOSE` formula can be useful in scenarios where you need to select values based on specific criteria or conditions.

CONCATENATE

Certainly! The CONCATENATE formula in Excel is used to **combine (concatenate) multiple text strings into a single string**. Here's a practical example:

Let's say you have a dataset with first names in column A and last names in column B, and you want to create a list of full names in column C.

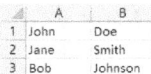

You can use the CONCATENATE formula to combine the first name and last name into a full name. Here's how you would do it:

1. In cell C1, enter the following formula: **=CONCATENATE(A1, " ", B1)**. This formula concatenates the contents of cell A1, a space (" "), and the contents of cell B1.

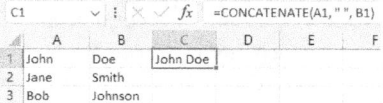

2. Drag the fill handle (a small square at the bottom-right corner of the cell) down to fill the formula for the entire column C.

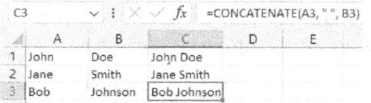

Alternatively, you can use the "**&**" operator as a shorthand for CONCATENATE: **=A1 & " " & B1**

This formula achieves the same result as the CONCATENATE formula.

After applying the formula, column C will contain the full names:

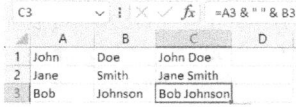

So, the practical application here is using CONCATENATE (or the "&" operator) to combine text from different cells into a single cell, which can be useful for creating full names, addresses, or any other concatenated strings in your Excel workbook.

COUNT

The COUNT formula in Excel is used to count the **number of cells that contain numbers within a specified range**. Here's a practical example:

Let's say you have a column of sales data in column A, and you want to find out how many sales transactions have been recorded. The data looks like this:

	A
1	$100
2	$150
3	
4	$80
5	$200

To count the number of sales transactions (cells that contain numbers), you can use the COUNT formula. Here's how you would do it:

1. Select the cell where you want the result to appear. Let's say you want the result in cell **B1**.
2. Type the following formula: **=COUNT(A1:A5)**

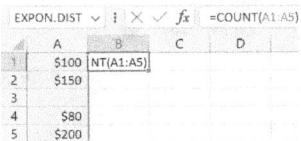

3. Press **Enter**.

The formula **=COUNT(A1:A5)** counts the number of cells in the range A1 to A5 that contain numbers.

The result in cell B1 will be:

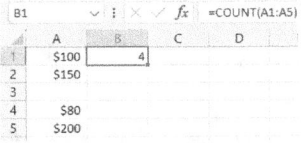

So, the practical application here is using the COUNT formula to quickly determine the number of sales transactions recorded in the given range. This is just one example, and COUNT can be used in various scenarios to count cells based on specific criteria within a range.

COUNTA

The COUNTA formula in Excel is used to **count the number of cells that are not empty** within a specified range. It counts all cells that contain any type of data, including numbers, text, errors, or logical values. Here's a practical example:

Let's say you have a worksheet with a list of products in column A, and you want to find out how many products are listed. The data looks like this:

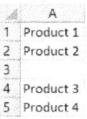

To count the number of products (non-empty cells), you can use the COUNTA formula. Here's how you would do it:

1. Select the cell where you want the result to appear. Let's say you want the result in cell B1.
2. Type the following formula: **=COUNTA(A1:A5)**
3. Press **Enter**.

The formula **=COUNTA(A1:A5)** counts the number of non-empty cells in the range A1 to A5. The result in cell B1 will be:

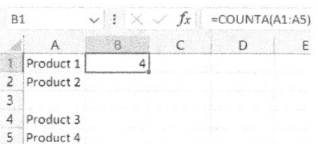

So, the practical application here is using the COUNTA formula to quickly determine the number of products listed in the given range. This formula is handy when you want to count cells with any type of data, not just numeric values.

COUNTIF

The COUNTIF formula in Excel is used to count the **number of cells that meet a specific condition within a given range**. Here's a practical example:

Suppose you have a list of exam scores in column A, and you want to count the number of students who scored higher than or equal to 80. The data looks like this:

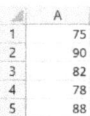

To count the number of scores equal to or greater than 80, you can use the COUNTIF formula. Here's how you would do it:

1. Select the cell where you want the result to appear. Let's say you want the result in cell B1.
2. Type the following formula: **=COUNTIF(A1:A5, ">=80")**
3. Press **Enter**.

The formula **=COUNTIF(A1:A5, ">=80")**` counts the number of cells in the range A1 to A5 that meet the condition "greater than or equal to 80."

The result in cell B1 will be:

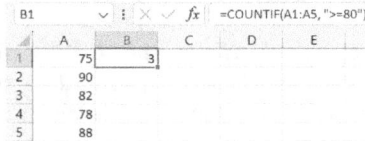

So, the practical application here is using the COUNTIF formula to quickly determine the number of students who scored equal to or higher than 80 in the given range. This formula is valuable when you need to count cells based on specific criteria within a range.

COUNTIFS

The COUNTIFS formula in Excel is used to count the **number of cells that meet multiple conditions within a given range**. Here's a practical example:

Suppose you have a dataset with student names in column A, scores in column B, and you want to count the number of students who scored higher than 80 in a specific subject. The data looks like this:

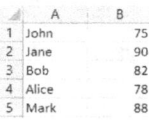

To count the number of students who scored higher than 80 in a specific subject (let's say, subject C), you can use the COUNTIFS formula. Here's how you would do it:

1. Select the cell where you want the result to appear. Let's say you want the result in cell C1.
2. Type the following formula: **=COUNTIFS(B1:B5, ">80")**
3. Press **Enter**.

This formula counts the number of cells in the range B1 to B5 where the score is greater than 80. The result in cell C1 will be:

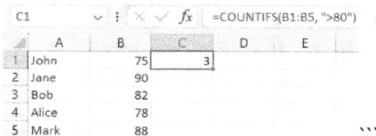

So, the practical application here is using the COUNTIFS formula to count the number of students who scored higher than 80 in a specific subject. This formula is useful when you have multiple conditions that you want to apply simultaneously.

DATE

The DATE formula in Excel is used to create a **date by specifying the year, month, and day** as separate arguments. Here's a practical example:

Suppose you want to create a worksheet that tracks project deadlines. You have the year, month, and day for each deadline in separate columns (e.g., column A for the year, column B for the month, and column C for the day). You can use the DATE formula to combine these values into a single date.

Assume you have the following data:

	A	B	C
1	2024	11	15
2	2024	12	1
3	2025	2	28

In column D, you can use the DATE formula to combine these values into a date. In cell D1, enter the following formula: **=DATE(A1, B1, C1)**

This formula takes the year from cell A1, the month from cell B1, and the day from cell C1 and creates a date. Drag the fill handle down to fill the formula for the entire column D.

The result will be:

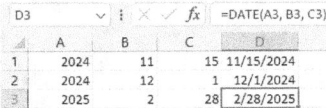

Now, column D contains the combined dates. This is just a simple example, and you can adjust the formula based on the structure of your data. The DATE formula is useful for creating date values dynamically based on separate year, month, and day components.

DAY

The DAY formula in Excel is used to extract the **day component** from a date. Here's a practical example:

Assume you have a column A with a list of dates:

	A
1	2/29/2024
2	6/7/2024
3	31/12/2024

Now, let's say you want to create a new column (let's say column B) that extracts the day component from each date. In cell B1, you can use the DAY formula as follows: =DAY(A1)

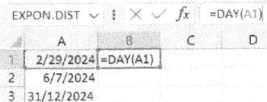

This formula extracts the day from the date in cell A1. Drag the fill handle down to fill the formula for the entire column B.

The result will be:

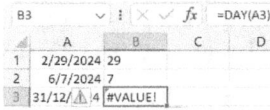

The formula expects a date in the format mm/dd/yyyy. This is the reason for the error message.

Now, column B contains the day component extracted from each date in column A.

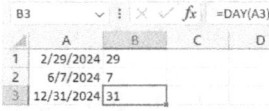

This is a simple example, and you can use the DAY formula in more complex scenarios where you need to work with the day component of dates in your Excel worksheet.

DAYS

The DAYS formula in Excel is used to calculates the **number of days between two dates**.

Suppose you have a start date in cell A1 and an end date in cell B1, and you want to calculate the number of days between these two dates. The data looks like this:

In cell C1, you can use the following formula to calculate the difference in days:

=DAYS(B1,A1)

This formula subtracts the start date in A1 from the end date in B1, giving you the difference in days.

The result will be:

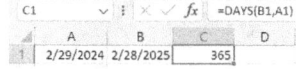

The value in cell C1 represents the number of days between the start date and end date.

Keep in mind that the result is a straightforward subtraction of dates, which assumes each day has a value of 1. If you want to exclude weekends or holidays, or if you want a more complex calculation, you might need to explore additional formulas or approaches.

EOMONTH

The EOMONTH formula in Excel is used to get the **last day of the month** that is a specified number of months before or after a specified date. Here's a practical example:

Assume you have a list of invoice dates in column A, and you want to calculate the due date, which is the last day of the month for each invoice date. The data looks like this:

In column B, you can use the EOMONTH formula to calculate the due date. In cell B1, enter the following formula: **=EOMONTH(A1, 0)**

This formula uses the EOMONTH formula to get the last day of the month for the date in cell A1. The second argument, `0`, means the same month. Drag the fill handle down to fill the formula for the entire column B.

The result will be:

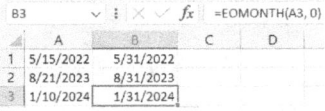

Now, column 3 contains the due dates, which are the last days of the months for the respective invoice dates.

This is a simple example, and you can customize the formula based on your specific needs. The EOMONTH formula is useful for scenarios where you need to calculate dates related to the end of a month.

EXP

The **EXP** formula in Excel is used to calculate the **exponential value of a number**, where the base of the exponent is the mathematical constant **e** (approximately 2.71828). Here's a practical example:

Let's say you have a dataset with growth rates, and you want to calculate the future values based on the exponential growth formula. The formula for exponential growth is:

Future value = Initial value * EXP(Growth rate * Time)

Assume you have the following data:

	A	B	C
1	Initial value	Growth rate	Time (years)
2	100	0.05	2
3	200	0.03	3
4	50	0.08	5

In column D, you can use the `EXP` formula to calculate the future values based on the exponential growth formula. In cell D2, enter the following formula: =A2 * EXP(B2 * C2)

This formula calculates the future value for the first row. Drag the fill handle down to fill the formula for the entire column D.

The result will be:

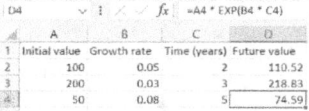

D4			f_x	=A4 * EXP(B4 * C4)	
	A	B	C	D	
1	Initial value	Growth rate	Time (years)	Future value	
2	100	0.05	2	110.52	
3	200	0.03	3	218.83	
4	50	0.08	5	74.59	

Now, column D contains the calculated future values based on the exponential growth formula. This is just a simple example, and the **EXP** formula is often used in various mathematical and financial calculations where exponential growth or decay is involved.

FILTER

The FILTER formula is for **dynamic data filtering**.

Here's a simple example of how you might use the FILTER formula:

Suppose you have a dataset with a list of products in column A and their corresponding prices in column B. You want to filter the products that have prices higher than $50.

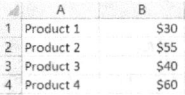

	A	B
1	Product 1	$30
2	Product 2	$55
3	Product 3	$40
4	Product 4	$60

1. In ce l D1, enter the criteria you want to filter by, for example, **$50**.
2. In cell E1, enter the following formula: **=FILTER(A1:B4, B1:B4 > D1)**. This formula uses the FILTER formula to filter the products and prices based on the condition that the price in column B is greater than the value in cell D1.
3. Press **Enter**.

The result will be:

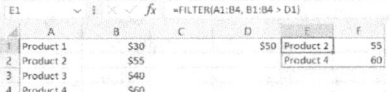

Now, column E contains the products and column F contains their corresponding prices, filtered based on the condition.

Keep in mind that the FILTER formula is available in Excel 365 or Excel 2021, and its usage may vary depending on your Excel version. If you are using an older version of Excel, you might need to use alternative methods such as using the "Filter" feature on the Data tab or using the IF or IFERROR formulas combined with other formulas for dynamic filtering.

FORMULATEXT

The FORMULATEXT formula in Excel is used to **extract and display the formula as text** from a specified cell. This can be useful for auditing or documentation purposes. Here's a practical example:

Suppose you have a formula in cell A1, and you want to display the formula as text in cell B1:

	A
1	5
2	8
3	3
4	6
5	2

Now, let's say you want to calculate the average of the numbers in column A in cell B1, and you want to display the formula as text in cell B2:

1. In cell B1, enter the formula to calculate the average: **=AVERAGE(A1:A5)**
2. In cell C1, use the FORMULATEXT formula to display the formula as text: **=FORMULATEXT(B1)**. Now, cell B1 calculates the average, and cell C1 displays the formula as text.

The result will be:

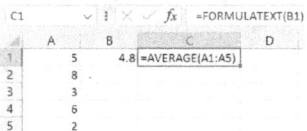

This way, you can use FORMULATEXT to display the formula in a cell as text. This can be particularly helpful when you want to document or share your worksheet while showing the underlying formulas. Keep in mind that FORMULATEXT is available in Excel 2013 and later versions.

FV

The FV (Future Value) formula in Excel is used to calculate the **future value of an investment** based on a series of periodic payments and a constant interest rate. Here's a practical example:

Suppose you are planning to save a certain amount of money every month for retirement. You want to calculate the future value of your monthly contributions given a fixed interest rate. Let's assume the following data:

- Monthly contribution: $500
- Annual interest rate: 6%
- Number of years: 20

In this example, the interest rate needs to be converted to a monthly rate, so the monthly contribution and the monthly interest rate will be used in the FV formula.

1. In cell A1, enter the monthly contribution: **500**.
2. In cell B2, enter the annual interest rate: **6%**.
3. In cell A2, enter the number of years: **20**.
4. In cell B2, calculate the monthly interest rate: **=B1/12**. This formula divides the annual interest rate by 12 to get the monthly rate.

5. In cell B3, calculate the total number of months: **=A2*12**. This formula multiplies the number of years by 12 to get the total number of months.
6. In cell B4, calculate the future value using the FV formula: **=FV(B2, B3, -A1)**. This formula uses the FV formula with the monthly interest rate, total number of months, and negative monthly contribution as arguments.

The result will be:

B4				fx	=FV(B2,B3,-A1)
	A	B	C		
1	$500	6%			
2	20	0.005			
3		240			
4		$231,020			

So, according to this calculation, if you save $500 every month with a 6% annual interest rate, after 20 years, the future value of your savings would be approximately $231,020. This is a simplified example, and you can adapt the FV formula to various scenarios depending on your specific needs.

HLOOKUP

The HLOOKUP formula in Excel is used to **search for a value in the first row of a range** (the header row) and return a value in the same column from a specified row. Here's a practical example:

Suppose you have a table of student scores with student names in the first column (column A), and you want to find the score of a specific student in a specific subject. The table looks like this:

	A	B	C	D
1	Student	Math	English	Science
2	John	85	92	88
3	Jane	90	85	92
4	Bob	78	80	85

In this example, let's say you want to find the score of Jane in English. You can use the HLOOKUP formula to accomplish this:

1. In cell E1, enter the student name you're interested in, let's say "Jane."
2. In cell E2, enter the subject you're interested in, let's say "English."
3. In cell E3, use the following HLOOKUP formula:

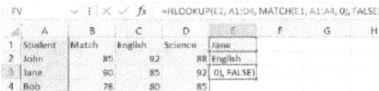

This formula looks for the subject specified in cell E2 (English) in the header row (A1:D1). It then uses the MATCH formula to find the row number corresponding to the student name specified in cell E1 (Jane) and adds 1 to get the correct row for the HLOOKUP. The FALSE argument indicates an exact match.

The result will be:

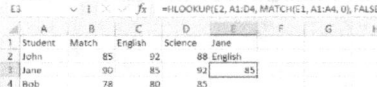

Now, cell E3 displays the score of Jane in English, which is 85.

This is a simple example, and you can adapt the HLOOKUP formula to different scenarios where you need to search for values in a horizontal header row.

HOUR

The HOUR formula in Excel is used to extract the **hour component from a given time**. Here's a practical example:

Let's say you have a list of timestamps in column A, and you want to extract the hour from each timestamp.

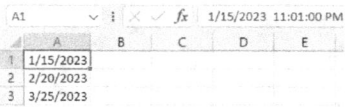

In this example, column A contains timestamps. In column B, you can use the HOUR formula to extract the hour from each timestamp. Assuming the timestamps are in the format "yyyy-mm-dd":

In cell B1, enter the following formula:

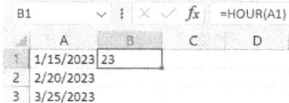

Drag the fill handle down to fill the formula for the entire column B.

The result will be:

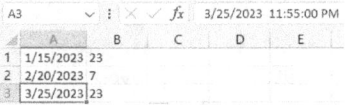

Note: The hour is displayed as "0" when the timestamps do not include a time component. If your timestamps include time, the HOUR formula will extract the corresponding hour.

HYPERLINK

The HYPERLINK formula in Excel is used to **create a clickable hyperlink** within a cell. Here's a practical example:

Let's say you have a list of websites in column A, and you want to create hyperlinks to these websites in column B.

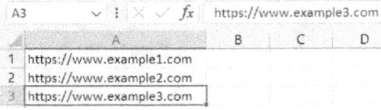

In this example, column A contains website URLs. In column B, you can use the HYPERLINK formula to create hyperlinks.

In cell B1, enter the following formula: **=HYPERLINK(A1, "Visit Example 1")**

This formula creates a hyperlink in cell B1 that points to the URL in cell A1, and the display text is set to "Visit Example 1."

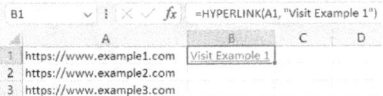

In cell B2, enter the following formula: **=HYPERLINK(A2, "Visit Example 2")** . In cell B3, enter the following formula: **=HYPERLINK(A3, "Visit Example 3")**. The result will be:

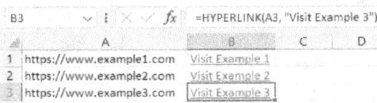

Now, column B contains clickable hyperlinks. When you click on any link in column B, it will open the corresponding website in your default web browser.

You can customize the display text by changing the second argument of the HYPERLINK formula. This allows you to have meaningful and descriptive link texts instead of displaying the full URL.

IF

The IF formula in Excel is commonly used for conditional logic, allowing you to **perform different actions based on whether a specified condition is true or false**. Here's a practical example:

Let's say you have a list of exam scores in column A, and you want to categorize each score as "Pass" or "Fail" based on a passing threshold.

	A
1	75
2	60
3	90

In this example, let's assume the passing threshold is 70. In column B, you can use the IF formula to categorize each score.

In cell B1, enter the following formula: **=IF(A1 >= 70, "Pass", "Fail")**

This formula checks if the score in cell A1 is greater than or equal to 70. If true, it returns "Pass"; otherwise, it returns "Fail."

Drag the fill handle down to fill the formula for the entire column B.

The result will be:

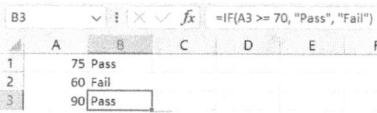

Now, column B categorizes each score as either "Pass" or "Fail" based on the specified passing threshold.

You can customize the conditions and the values returned based on your specific requirements. The IF formula is versatile and widely used for creating conditional statements in Excel.

IFERROR

The IFERROR formula in Excel is used to **handle errors in a formula** by providing a specific value or alternative calculation if an error occurs. Here's a practical example:

Let's say you have a list of numbers in column A, and you want to calculate the square root of each number. However, some numbers might be negative, resulting in an error. You can use the IFERROR formula to display a specific message for those cases.

	A
1	25
2	-9
3	16

In this example, column A contains numbers. In column B, you can use the IFERROR formula to calculate the square root and handle errors.

In cell B1, enter the following formula: **=IFERROR(SQRT(A1), "Invalid input")**

This formula attempts to calculate the square root of the number in cell A1. If successful, it returns the square root; otherwise, it returns the specified message "Invalid input."

Drag the fill handle down to fill the formula for the entire column B.

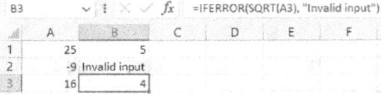

Now, column B calculates the square root for valid inputs and displays the message "Invalid input" for cases where an error occurs, such as attempting to calculate the square root of a negative number.

This is just one example, and you can customize the alternative value or message based on the specific error handling you need in your calculations. The IFERROR formula is useful for making your formulas more robust and user-friendly.

IFS

The IFS formula in Excel is used to perform multiple tests and **return a value corresponding to the first true condition**. Here's a practical example:

Let's say you have a list of exam scores in column A, and you want to assign grades based on different score ranges.

	A
1	85
2	60
3	95

In this example, let's set the following grade ranges:

- A: 90 and above
- B: 80 to 89
- C: 70 to 79
- D: 60 to 69
- F: Below 60

In cell B1, you can use the IFS formula to assign grades based on the score:

=IFS(A1 >= 90, "A", A1 >= 80, "B", A1 >= 70, "C", A1 >= 60, "D", A1 < 60, "F")

This formula checks each condition in order and returns the corresponding grade based on the score in cell A1.

Drag the fill handle down to fill the formula for the entire column B.

The result will be:

Now, column B assigns grades to each score based on the specified ranges using the IFS formula.

Note that IFS is available in Excel 365, Excel 2019, and later versions. If you're using an earlier version of Excel, you can achieve similar results using nested IF formulas, as shown in a previous example.

INDEX

The INDEX formula in Excel is used to **retrieve the value at a specific row and column intersection within a given range**. Here's a practical example:

Suppose you have a table with student names in column A, subjects in row 1, and corresponding scores in the cells:

	A	B	C	D
1		Match	English	Science
2	Student 1	85	92	88
3	Student 2	90	85	92
4	Student 3	78	80	85

Now, let's say you want to retrieve the score of "Student 2" in "English."

In cell E1, you can use the INDEX formula as follows:

=INDEX(B2:D4, MATCH("Student 2", A2:A4, 0), MATCH("English", B1:D1, 0))

This formula uses INDEX to look up the value within the range B2:D4. The row number is determined using the MATCH formula to find the position of "Student 2" in column A, and the column number is determined using the MATCH formula to find the position of "English" in the header row.

The result will be:

	A	B	C	D	E	F	G	H	I	J
E1					=INDEX(B2:D4, MATCH("Student 2", A2:A4, 0), MATCH("English", B1:D1, 0))					
1		Match	English	Science	85					
2	Student 1	85	92	88						
3	Student 2	90	85	92						
4	Student 3	78	80	85						

Now, cell E1 displays the score of "Student 2" in "English" using the INDEX formula.

You can customize the formula based on your specific table structure and data. The INDEX formula is versatile and widely used for dynamic lookups within tables in Excel.

INDIRECT

The INDIRECT formula in Excel is used to **convert a text string into a cell reference, making it useful for creating dynamic references**. Here's an example where INDIRECT is used to dynamically reference a specific cell based on user input.

Suppose you have a list of sales data with product names in column A, and you want to allow the user to input a product name in cell D1. You then want to use INDIRECT to dynamically reference the total sales for that specific product.

	A	B
1	Product 1	$100
2	Product 2	$150
3	Product 3	$120

Now, in cell D1, the user can input the product name they want to check, for example, "Product 2".

In cell E1, you can use the INDIRECT formula to dynamically reference the total sales for the specified product:

=INDIRECT("B" & MATCH(D1, A:A, 0))

This formula works as follows:

- The MATCH formula (`MATCH(D1, A:A, 0)`) finds the position of the input product name in column A.
- The `&` operator concatenates the result with the column letter "B" to create a text string like "B2", "B3", etc.
- The INDIRECT formula then interprets this text string as a cell reference, dynamically referencing the cell containing the total sales for the specified product.

If the user inputs "Product 2" in cell D1, the formula in cell E1 will dynamically reference cell B2 and display the corresponding total sales value:

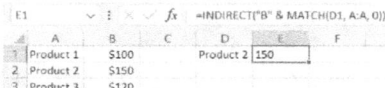

Now, cell E1 dynamically displays the total sales for the product specified in cell D1 using INDIRECT. This can be particularly useful for creating interactive dashboards or reports where users can select specific criteria.

INT

The INT formula in Excel is used to **round a number down to the nearest integer**. Here's an example where INT is applied to round down a decimal value to the nearest whole number.

Suppose you have a list of prices in column A, and you want to round down each price to the nearest whole number.

	A
1	$15.75
2	$22.30
3	$9.99

In this example, you can use the INT formula to round down each price in column A.

In cell B1, enter the following formula:

=INT(A1)

This formula applies the INT formula to round down the price in cell A1 to the nearest whole number.

Drag the fill handle down to fill the formula for the entire column B.

The result will be:

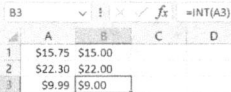

Now, column B contains the prices rounded down to the nearest whole number using the INT formula.

This is a simple example, and you can adapt the INT formula based on your specific requirements. The INT formula is useful for scenarios where you need to work with whole numbers and discard the decimal part of a number.

IRR

The IRR (Internal Rate of Return) formula in Excel is used to calculate the **internal rate of return for a series of cash flows**. Here's an example where IRR is applied to determine the internal rate of return for an investment.

Suppose you have an investment where you are investing $1,000 in Year 0, receiving $500 in Year 1, and $600 in Year 2. You want to calculate the internal rate of return for this investment.

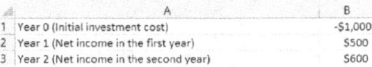

In this example, you can use the IRR formula to calculate the internal rate of return.

In cell B4, enter the following formula:

=IRR(B1:B3)

This formula applies the IRR formula to the cash flow values in cells B1 to B3.

The result will be:

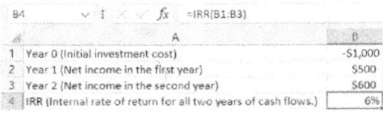

Now, cell B4 displays the internal rate of return for the investment, which is approximately 6%.

Keep in mind that the IRR formula assumes that cash flows occur at regular intervals. If the cash flows are irregular, you may need to use the XIRR formula instead. The IRR is commonly used in financial analysis to evaluate the profitability of an investment.

ISBLANK

The ISBLANK formula in Excel is used to **check if a cell is blank or empty**. Here's an example where ISBLANK is applied to find empty cells based on their content.

Suppose you have a list of tasks in column A, and you want to highlight the tasks that do not have a due date specified in column B.

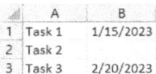

In this example, you can use the ISBLANK formula to conditionally format cells in column B.

1. Select the cells B1.
2. Enter the following formula: **=ISBLANK(B1)**
3. Drag the fill handle down to fill the formula for the entire column B.
4. The result will be:

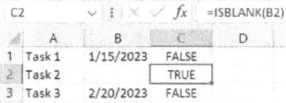

Cells in column B can be conditionally formatted.

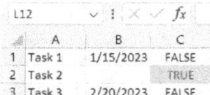

This is a simple example, and you can customize the formatting and conditions based on your specific needs. The ISBLANK formula is useful for checking the presence or absence of data in cells.

ISERROR

The ISERROR formula in Excel is used to **check whether a cell contains an error**. Here's an example where ISERROR is applied to identify and handle errors in a formula.

Suppose you have a division calculation in column C, and you want to check if any errors (such as #DIV/0!) occur in the results.

	A	B
1	10	2
2	15	0
3	20	5

In this example, you want to perform the division in column C and use ISERROR to identify cells with errors.

In cell C1, enter the following division formula: **=A1/B1**

This formula calculates the result of dividing cell A1 by cell B1.

C1				f_x	=A1/B1
	A	B	C	D	
1	10	2	5		
2	15	0			
3	20	5			

In cell D1, use the ISERROR formula to check if an error occurs in cell C1: **=ISERROR(C1)**

D1				f_x	=ISERROR(C1)
	A	B	C	D	
1	10	2	5	FALSE	
2	15	0			
3	20	5			

This formula returns TRUE if an error occurs in cell C1; otherwise, it returns FALSE.

Drag the fill handle down to fill the formula for the entire column C and D.

The result will be:

O22				f_x	
	A	B	C	D	
1	10	2	5	FALSE	
2	15	0	#DIV/0!	TRUE	
3	20	5	4	FALSE	

Now, column D indicates whether an error occurs in the corresponding cell in column C. You can use this information to handle errors or conditionally format cells.

For instance, you might use the IF and ISERROR formulas together to display a custom message when an error occurs. In cell E1, you could enter:

=IF(ISERROR(C1), "Error occurred", C1)

This formula checks if there's an error in cell C1. If true, it displays "Error occurred"; otherwise, it shows the result.

The result will be:

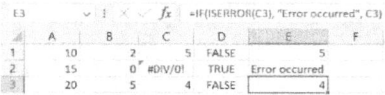

This way, you can identify and handle errors in your calculations using ISERROR.

ISNUMBER

The ISNUMBER formula in Excel is used to **check whether a cell contains a numeric value**. Here's an example where ISNUMBER is applied to identify cells with numeric values in a range.

Suppose you have a list of data in column A, and you want to highlight cells that contain numeric values.

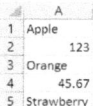

In cell B1 enter the following formula: **=ISNUMBER(A1)**

Drag the fill handle down to fill the formula for the entire column B.

The result will be:

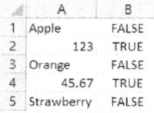

You can use conditional formatting. Now, cells in column B cell in this same row contain numeric values are highlighted based on the ISNUMBER condition.

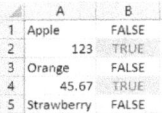

This is a simple example, and you can customize the formatting and conditions based on your specific needs. The ISNUMBER formula is useful for checking if a cell contains a numeric value in various scenarios.

ISTEXT

The ISTEXT formula in Excel is used to **check whether a cell contains text**. Here's an example where ISTEXT is applied to identify cells with text values in a range.

Suppose you have a list of data in column A, and you want to highlight cells that contain text values.

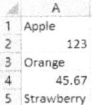

In cell B1 enter the following formula: **=ISTEXT(A1)**

Drag the fill handle down to fill the formula for the entire column B.

The result will be:

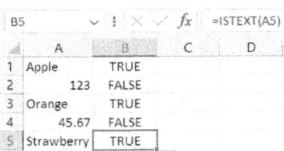

You can use conditional formatting. Now, cells in column B cell in this same row contain numeric values are highlighted based on the ISTEXT condition.

	A	B
1	Apple	TRUE
2	123	FALSE
3	Orange	TRUE
4	45.67	FALSE
5	Strawberry	TRUE

This is a simple example, and you can customize the formatting and conditions based on your specific needs. The ISTEXT formula is useful for checking if a cell contains text in various scenarios.

LEFT

Returns a specified number of characters from the beginning of a text string.

LEN

The LEFT and RIGHT formulas in Excel are used to **extract a specified number of characters from the left or right side of a text string**, respectively. Here's an example where LEFT and RIGHT are applied to extract portions of text from a column.

Suppose you have a list of product codes in column A, and you want to extract the first three characters (LEFT) and the last four characters (RIGHT) of each code.

In this example, you can use the LEFT and RIGHT formulas to extract portions of the product codes.

In cell B1, enter the following formula to extract the first three characters:

=LEFT(A1, 3)

This formula extracts the leftmost three characters from the product code in cell A1.

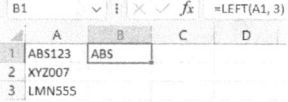

In cell C1, enter the following formula to extract the last four characters:

=RIGHT(A1, 4)

This formula extracts the rightmost four characters from the product code in cell A1.

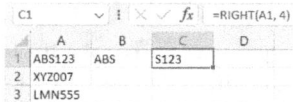

Drag the fill handle down to fill the formulas for the entire columns B and C.

The result will be:

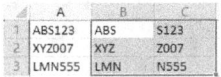

Now, columns B and C contain the extracted portions of text from the product codes. The LEFT formula is used to extract the first three characters, and the RIGHT formula is used to extract the last four characters.

You can adjust the number of characters as needed for your specific requirements. These formulas are particularly useful when you need to work with substrings within text data.

LOG

The LOG formula in Excel is used to calculate the **decimal logarithm of a number** to base 10. Here's an example where the LOG formula is applied to find the logarithm of numbers in a column.

Suppose you have a list of numbers in column A, and you want to calculate the natural logarithm (base e) of each number.

	A
1	1
2	10
3	100

In this example, you can use the LOG formula to calculate the logarithm of the numbers in column A.

In cell B1, enter the following formula to calculate the natural logarithm:

=LOG(A1)

This formula calculates the decimal logarithm of the number in cell A1 to the base 10.

Drag the fill handle down to fill the formula for the entire column B.

The result will be:

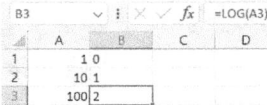

Now, column B contains the natural logarithm of the numbers in column A. The LOG formula is applied to each number individually.

You can also specify a different base. For example, if you want to calculate the natural logarithm of numbers in base e, you can use:

=LN(A1)

This would calculate the logarithm of the number in cell A1 to the base 2.

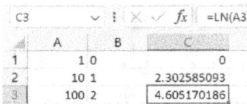

Adjust the formula based on your specific requirements and the base you need for the logarithm.

You can also specify a different base for the logarithm by providing a second argument to the LOG formula. For example, if you want to calculate the logarithm of numbers in base 2, you can use: =LOG(A1, 2).

LOWER

The LOWER formula in Excel is used to **convert text to lowercase**. Here's an example where LOWER is applied to convert uppercase names in a column to lowercase.

Suppose you have a list of names in column A, and you want to convert all the letters to lowercase.

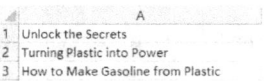

In this example, you can use the LOWER formula to convert the words in column A to lowercase.

In cell B1, enter the following formula: **=LOWER(A1)**

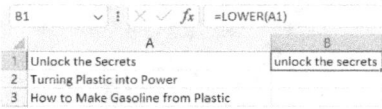

This formula converts the text in cell A1 to lowercase.

Drag the fill handle down to fill the formula for the entire column B.

The result will be:

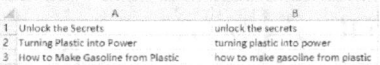

Now, column B contains the words converted to lowercase using the LOWER formula.

You can use this formula to standardize text or perform case-insensitive comparisons in your data. Adjust the formula based on your specific needs and the cells you want to convert to lowercase.

MATCH

The MATCH formula in Excel is used to **search for a specified value** in a range and return the relative position of that item. Here's an example where MATCH is applied to find the position of a product in a list.

Suppose you have a list of products in column A, and you want to find the position of a specific product, let's say "365."

	A
1	363
2	364
3	365
4	366

In this example, you can use the MATCH formula to find the position of "365" in column A.

In cell B1, enter the following formula: **=MATCH(365, A:A,0)**

This formula searches for the value "365" in column A and returns the relative position of that item. The third argument, `0`, indicates an exact match.

The result will be:

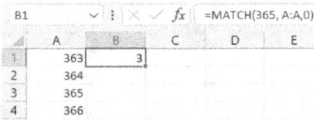

You can use the MATCH formula in various scenarios, such as looking up values in a table, validating data, or creating dynamic formulas based on the position of an item in a range. Adjust the formula based on your specific needs and the range you are working with.

MATCH and INDEX

The combination of MATCH and INDEX formulas in Excel is a powerful way to perform advanced lookups. Here's an example where MATCH and INDEX are applied together to **retrieve information based on a specific criteria**.

Suppose you have a table of products with their prices in columns A and B, and you want to find the price of a specific product, let's say "Orange."

	A	B
1	Apple	1.5
2	Orange	2.1
3	Strawberry	2.5
4	Banana	1.75

Now, let's say you want to find the price of "Orange" using the MATCH and INDEX combination.

In cell C1, enter the following formula:

=INDEX(B:B, MATCH("Orange", A:A, 0))

This formula works as follows:

- The MATCH formula (`MATCH("Orange", A:A, 0)`) finds the position of "Orange" in column A.
- The INDEX formula (`INDEX(B:B, row_number)`) then uses this position to retrieve the corresponding price from column B.

The result will be:

C1				fx	=INDEX(B:B, MATCH("Orange", A:A, 0))	
	A	B	C	D	E	F
1	Apple	1.5	2.1			
2	Orange	2.1				
3	Strawberry	2.5				
4	Banana	1.75				

Now, cell C2 contains the price of "Orange," which is 2.1.

This combination of MATCH and INDEX is particularly useful when you need to look up a value based on a specific criterion, and it offers more flexibility than traditional lookup formulas like VLOOKUP or HLOOKUP. Adjust the formula based on your specific table structure and data.

44

MAX

The MAX formula in Excel is used to find the **largest value in a range of cells**. Here's an example where the MAX formula is applied to find the highest sales amount in a list.

Suppose you have a list of numbers in column A, and you want to find the maximum number.

In this example, you can use the MAX formula to find the highest amount.

In cell B1, enter the following formula: **=MAX(A1:A4)**

This formula uses the MAX formula to find the maximum value in the range A1 to A4.

The result will be:

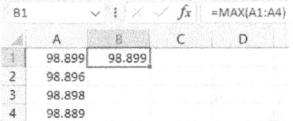

Now, cell B1 contains the maximum amount, which is 98.899.

You can use the MAX formula in various scenarios, such as finding the highest score in a list of exam results, determining the peak temperature in a set of daily temperatures, and more. Adjust the formula based on the range of cells you want to analyze.

MIN

The MIN formula in Excel is used to find the **smallest value in a range of cells**. Here's an example where the MIN formula is applied to find the minimum value in a list.

Suppose you have a list of numbers in column A, and you want to find the minimum number.

	A
1	98.899
2	98.896
3	98.898
4	98.889

In this example, you can use the MIN formula to find the minimum amount.

In cell B1, enter the following formula: **=MIN(A1:A4)**

This formula uses the MIN formula to find the minimum value in the range A1 to A4.

The result will be:

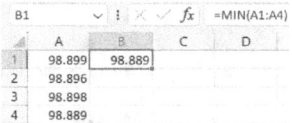

Now, cell B1 contains the minimum amount, which is 98.889.

You can use the MIN formula in various scenarios, such as finding the lowest temperature in a set of daily temperatures, determining the minimum score in a list of exam results, and more. Adjust the formula based on the range of cells you want to analyze.

MINUTE

The MINUTE formula in Excel is used to **extract the minutes from a given time**. Here's an example where the MINUTE formula is applied to extract the minutes from a list of time values.

Suppose you have a list of time values in column A, and you want to extract the minutes from each time.

	A
1	10:30 AM
2	3:45 PM
3	12:16 PM
4	9:00 AM

In this example, you can use the MINUTE formula to extract the minutes from the time values.

In cell B1, enter the following formula: **=MINUTE(A1)**

This formula uses the MINUTE formula to extract the minutes from the time in cell A1.

Drag the fill handle down to fill the formula for the entire column B.

The result will be:

	A	B	C	D
1	10:30 AM	30		
2	3:45 PM	45		
3	12:16 PM	16		
4	9:00 AM	0		

B4 =MINUTE(A4)

Now, column B contains the minutes extracted from the time values in column A.

You can use the MINUTE formula in various scenarios, such as calculating the duration of events, analyzing time-based data, and more. Adjust the formula based on your specific needs and the range of cells you want to analyze.

MOD

The MOD formula in Excel is used to find the **remainder after division of one number by another**. Here's an example where the MOD formula is applied to calculate the remainder when dividing a list of numbers by a specified divisor.

Suppose you have a list of numbers in column A, and you want to find the remainder when each number is divided by 5.

	A
1	10
2	17
3	22
4	8

In this example, you can use the MOD formula to calculate the remainder when each number in column A is divided by 5.

In cell B1, enter the following formula: **=MOD(A1, 5)**

This formula uses the MOD formula to find the remainder when the number in cell A1 is divided by 5.

Drag the fill handle down to fill the formula for the entire column B.

The result will be:

	A	B	C	D
1	10	0		
2	17	2		
3	22	2		
4	8	3		

B4 =MOD(A4, 5)

Now, column B contains the remainder when each number in column A is divided by 5.

You can use the MOD formula in various scenarios, such as identifying patterns in sequences, creating repeating patterns, and more. Adjust the formula based on your specific needs and the divisor you want to use for the remainder calculation.

MONTH

The MONTH formula in Excel is used to **extract the month from a date**. Here's an example where the MONTH formula is applied to extract the month from a list of dates.

Suppose you have a list of dates in column A, and you want to extract the month from each date.

In this example, you can use the MONTH formula to extract the month from the date values.

In cell B1, enter the following formula: **=MONTH(A1)**

This formula uses the MONTH formula to extract the month from the date in cell A1.

Drag the fill handle down to fill the formula for the entire column B.

The result will be:

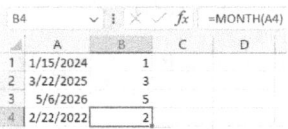

Now, column B contains the month extracted from each date in column A.

You can use the MONTH formula to analyze trends over months, group data by month, or perform other date-related calculations. Adjust the formula based on your specific needs and the range of cells you want to analyze.

NETWORKDAYS

The NETWORKDAYS formula in Excel is used to calculate the **number of whole workdays (Monday through Friday) between two dates**, excluding specified holidays. Here's an example where the NETWORKDAYS formula is applied to calculate the number of workdays between two dates, excluding holidays.

Suppose you have a start date in cell A1, an end date in cell B1, and a list of holidays in cells D1 to D3.

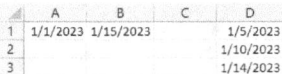

In this example, you want to calculate the number of workdays between the start date (A1) and end date (B1), excluding the specified holidays in column D.

In cell C1, enter the following formula: **=NETWORKDAYS(A1, B1, D1:D3)**

This formula uses the NETWORKDAYS formula to calculate the number of workdays between the start date in cell A1 and the end date in cell B1, excluding the holidays specified in the range D1:D3.

The result will be:

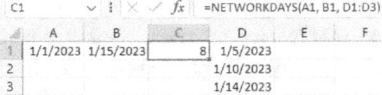

Now, cell C1 contains the number of workdays between the start date and end date, excluding the specified holidays.

You can adjust the formula based on your specific needs and the range of cells containing the holidays. The NETWORKDAYS formula is useful for calculating durations excluding weekends and holidays in business scenarios.

NOT

The NOT formula in Excel is used to **reverse the logical value** of its argument. It converts `TRUE` to `FALSE` and `FALSE` to `TRUE`. Here's an example where the NOT formula is applied to reverse the logical values in a list.

Suppose you have a list of logical values in column A, and you want to reverse these values using the NOT formula.

	A
1	TRUE
2	FALSE

In this example, you can use the NOT formula to reverse the logical values in column A.

In cell B1, enter the following formula: **=NOT(A1)**

This formula uses the NOT formula to reverse the logical value in cell A1.

Drag the fill handle down to fill the formula for the entire column B.

The result will be:

B2				fx	=NOT(A2)
	A	B	C	D	
1	TRUE	FALSE			
2	FALSE	TRUE			

Now, column B contains the reversed logical values using the NOT formula.

You can use the NOT formula in various scenarios, such as creating conditional formulas, validating data, or negating logical conditions. Adjust the formula based on your specific needs and the range of cells you want to reverse.

NOW

The NOW formula in Excel is used to insert the **current date and time** into a cell. However, it's important to note that the NOW formula is volatile, meaning it updates every time there is a change in the worksheet. Here's an example where the NOW formula is used to display the current date and time.

In a cell, enter the following formula: **=NOW()**

Press **Enter**, and the cell will display the current date and time.

=NOW()
D
12/3/2023 12:54

If you want to display only the date or time portion, you can use additional formulas to extract that information.

For example, to display only the current date, you can use the following formula:

=TODAY()

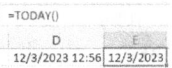

This formula, like NOW, is also volatile but only updates when there's a change in the worksheet.

If you want to display only the current time, you can use the following formula:

=TEXT(NOW(), "hh:mm AM/PM")

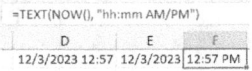

This formula uses the TEXT formula to format the current time in the desired format.

Remember that when using NOW or TODAY, the displayed value will update automatically when the worksheet is recalculated. If you want to capture the current date and time at a specific moment and prevent it from updating, you might consider copying and pasting the value as a static timestamp.

NPER

The NPER formula in Excel is used to calculate the number of payment periods for an investment based on periodic, constant payments and a constant interest rate. Here's an example where the NPER formula is applied to **determine the number of periods required to pay off a loan**.

Suppose you have a loan amount, an annual interest rate, and a fixed monthly payment, and you want to find out how many months it will take to pay off the loan.

Let's say you have the following data:

- Loan amount: $10,000 (cell A1)
- Annual interest rate: 5% (cell B1)
- Monthly payment: -$200 (negative because it's an outgoing payment, cell C1)

In cell D1, enter the following formula to calculate the number of payment periods (months) using the NPER formula: **=NPER(B1/12, C1, A1)**

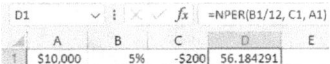

This formula uses the NPER formula to calculate the number of payment periods based on the monthly interest rate (B1/12), the monthly payment (C1), and the loan amount (A1).

The result will be the number of periods required to pay off the loan. Drag the fill handle down to extend the formula for multiple scenarios.

In this example, it would take approximately 57 months to pay off the loan with a fixed monthly payment of $200 and an annual interest rate of 5%.

You can adjust the values in cells A1, B1, and C1 to reflect different loan scenarios and see how the number of payment periods changes accordingly.

NPV

The NPV (Net Present Value) formula in Excel is used to calculate the present value of a series of cash flows. Here's an example where the NPV formula is applied to evaluate the **net present value of an investment**.

Suppose you have the following cash flows for an investment:

- Initial investment: -$10,000 (cell A1)
- Cash flow in Year 1: $3,000 (cell B1)
- Cash flow in Year 2: $4,000 (cell C1)
- Cash flow in Year 3: $5,000 (cell D1)
- Discount rate: 8% (cell E1)

In cell F1, enter the following formula to calculate the NPV:

=NPV(E1, B1:D1) + A1

This formula uses the NPV formula to calculate the net present value of the cash flows (B1:D1) discounted at the rate specified in cell E1. The initial investment (A1) is added to the result.

The result will be the net present value of the investment. Drag the fill handle down to extend the formula for multiple scenarios.

The result might look like this:

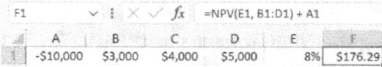

In this example, the net present value of the investment, taking into account the initial investment and future cash flows discounted at 8%, is approximately $176.

You can adjust the values in cells A1 to E1 to model different investment scenarios and evaluate the net present value accordingly.

OFFSET

The OFFSET formula in Excel is used to return a **reference that is offset from a starting cell or range of cells**. Here's an example where the OFFSET formula is applied to dynamically reference a range of cells.

Suppose you have a list of values in column A, and you want to dynamically reference a range of cells starting from a specified cell and extending for a certain number of rows and columns.

Let's say you have the following data:

In this example, you can use the OFFSET formula to dynamically reference a range of cells.

In cell B1, enter the following formula: **=SUM(OFFSET(A1, 0, 0, 3, 1))**

This formula uses the OFFSET formula to create a reference starting from cell A1, with zero rows and zero columns offset (meaning starting from A1 itself), and extending for 3 rows and 1 column. The SUM formula then calculates the sum of the values in this dynamically referenced range.

The result will be:

Now, cell B1 contains the sum of the values in the dynamically referenced range (A1:A3).

Let's break down the formula `=SUM(OFFSET($A$1, 0, 0, 3, 1))`:

- **SUM**: This is the Excel SUM formula, which is used to add up a range of numbers.
- **OFFSET(A1, 0, 0, 3, 1)**: This is the OFFSET formula, which returns a reference that is offset from a starting cell or range of cells.
- **A1**: This is the starting cell. The OFFSET formula starts from cell A1.
- **0, 0**: These are the row and column offsets. In this case, both are set to 0, meaning there is no offset from the starting cell in terms of rows or columns.
- **3, 1**: These are the height and width of the range to be returned. In this case, the range is 3 rows tall and 1 column wide.

So, the OFFSET formula essentially returns a reference to the range A1:A3 (3 rows, 1 column starting from A1).

The entire formula is using this dynamically referenced range as an argument to the SUM formula. It's summing up the values in the range A1:A3.

Let's go step by step:

1. OFFSET(A1, 0, 0, 3, 1): Returns the reference to the range A1:A3.
2. SUM(OFFSET(A1, 0, 0, 3, 1)): Adds up the values in the range A1:A3.

Assuming the values in A1:A3 are $100, $150, and $120, the result of this formula would be $370 (100 + 150 + 120).

You can adjust the parameters of the OFFSET formula based on your specific needs, such as changing the starting cell, the number of rows and columns to offset, and use it in various scenarios where dynamic referencing is required.

OR

The OR formula in Excel is used to test multiple conditions, and it **returns TRUE if at least one of the conditions is TRUE**. Here's an example where the OR formula is applied to check if at least one of two conditions is met.

Suppose you have a list of exam scores in column A, and you want to check if a student has passed. In this example, passing is defined as a score of 70 or higher.

	A
1	65
2	82
3	60
4	75

In this scenario, you can use the OR formula to check if a student has passed (score is 70 or higher).

In cell B1, enter the following formula: **=OR(A1>=70, A1>=70)**

This formula uses the OR formula to check if the score in cell A1 is greater than or equal to 70. The result will be TRUE if the condition is met, and FALSE otherwise.

Drag the fill handle down to extend the formula for the entire column B.

The result will be:

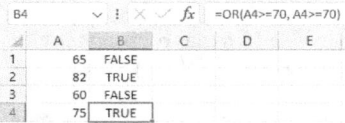

Now, column B contains TRUE for scores that are 70 or higher and FALSE for scores below 70.

You can adjust the formula based on your specific conditions and use the OR formula to check multiple conditions simultaneously.

PI

The PI formula in Excel returns the mathematical **constant Pi (π)**, which is approximately equal to 3.141592653589793. You can use it in formulas for calculations that involve circular or trigonometric formulas.

Here's a simple example:

In cell D1, you can enter the formula: **=PI()**

Press **Enter**, and the result will be the value of Pi:

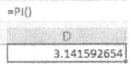

This value is the numerical representation of Pi, and you can use it in various mathematical calculations within your Excel workbook. For example, you might use it in formulas involving geometry, trigonometry, or physics.

PMT

The PMT formula in Excel is used to calculate the **monthly payment for a loan based on constant payments and a constant interest rate**. Here's an example where the PMT formula is applied to calculate the monthly payment for a loan.

Suppose you have the following data:

- Loan amount: $10,000 (cell A1)
- Annual interest rate: 5% (cell B1)
- Loan term in years: 3 (cell C1)

In cell D1, enter the following formula to calculate the monthly payment using the PMT formula: **=PMT(B1/12, C1*12, -A1)**

This formula uses the PMT formula to calculate the monthly payment. Here's a breakdown of the arguments:

- **B1/12**: Monthly interest rate, calculated by dividing the annual interest rate by 12.
- **C1*12**: Total number of payments, calculated by multiplying the number of years by 12 (months in a year).
- **-A1**: Loan amount, with a negative sign because it represents an outgoing payment.

The result will be the monthly payment for the loan. Drag the fill handle down to extend the formula for multiple scenarios.

The result might look like this:

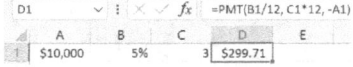

In this example, the monthly payment for a $10,000 loan with a 5% annual interest rate and a 3-year term is approximately -$300.

You can adjust the values in cells A1, B1, and C1 to model different loan scenarios and calculate the monthly payment accordingly.

POWER

The POWER formula in Excel is used to calculate a **number raised to a power**. Here's an example where the POWER formula is applied to calculate the square and cube of a set of numbers.

Suppose you have a list of numbers in column A, and you want to calculate their squares and cubes.

	A
1	2
2	3
3	4
4	5

In this example, you can use the POWER formula to calculate the squares and cubes of the numbers in column A.

In cell B1, enter the following formula to calculate the squares: **=POWER(A1, 2)**

This formula uses the POWER formula to raise the number in cell A1 to the power of 2 (calculating the square).

In cell C1, enter the following formula to calculate the cubes: **=POWER(A1, 3)**

This formula uses the POWER formula to raise the number in cell A1 to the power of 3 (calculating the cube).

Drag the fill handle down to extend the formulas for the entire column.

The result will be:

C4		f_x	=POWER(A4, 3)	
	A	B	C	D
1	2	4	8	
2	3	9	27	
3	4	16	64	
4	5	25	125	

Now, columns B and C contain the squares and cubes, respectively, of the numbers in column A.

You can adjust the formulas based on your specific needs and use the POWER formula to calculate values raised to different powers.

PROPER

The PROPER formula in Excel is used to convert text to proper case, which means the **first letter of each word is capitalized**, and the rest of the letters are in lowercase. Here's an example where the PROPER formula is applied to convert names to proper case.

Suppose you have a list of names in column A, and you want to convert them to proper case.

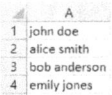

In this example, you can use the PROPER formula to convert the names to proper case.

In cell B1, enter the following formula: **=PROPER(A1)**

This formula uses the PROPER formula to convert the text in cell A1 to proper case.

Drag the fill handle down to extend the formula for the entire column.

The result will be:

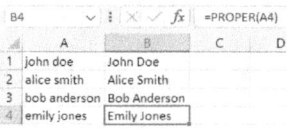

Now, column B contains the names converted to proper case using the PROPER formula.

You can use the PROPER formula to format text data in a way that makes it more readable, especially when dealing with names, titles, or other text where proper capitalization is desired. Adjust the formula based on the specific cells or range you want to convert.

PV

The PV (Present Value) formula in Excel is used to calculate the **present value of an investment**, based on a series of future cash flows and a discount rate.

Here's an example where the PV formula is applied to evaluate the present value of future cash flows.

Suppose you have the following data for an investment:

- Future cash flow in Year 1: $300 (cell B1)
- Future cash flow in Year 2: $400 (cell B2)
- Future cash flow in Year 3: $500 (cell B3)
- Discount rate: 8% (cell C1)

In cell D1, enter the following formula to calculate the present value using the PV formula:

=PV(C1, 1, 0, -B1) + PV(C1, 2, 0, -B2) + PV(C1, 3, 0, -B3)

This formula uses the PV formula to calculate the present value for each future cash flow and then adds them up. Here's a breakdown of the arguments:

- **C1**: Discount rate (annual rate of interest).
- **1, 2, 3**: The periods for each cash flow (Year 1, Year 2, Year 3).
- **0**: This argument is set to 0 because the cash flows are assumed to occur at the end of each period.
- **-B1, -B2, -B3**: The future cash flows with a negative sign since they represent outgoing payments.

The result will be the present value of the future cash flows. Drag the fill handle down to extend the formula for multiple scenarios.

The result might look like this:

In this example, the present value of the future cash flows, taking into account the discount rate of 8%, is approximately $10,176.

You can adjust the values in cells B1, B2, B3, and C1 to model different investment scenarios and calculate the present value accordingly.

RAND

The RAND formula in Excel is used to generate a **random decimal number** between 0 and 1. Here's a simple example of using the RAND formula:

Suppose you want to generate a random decimal number in each cell of a column, say from A1 to A5. You can use the RAND formula as follows:

In cell A1, enter the formula: **=RAND()**

Drag the fill handle down from the bottom-right corner of cell A1 to A5 to fill the cells with random decimal numbers.

The result might look like this:

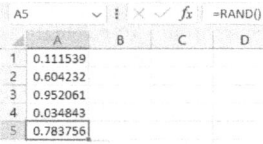

Every time you make a change to the worksheet or recalculate, Excel will generate new random decimal numbers.

If you want to generate random decimal numbers within a specific range, you can use the following formula:

=MIN_VALUE + (MAX_VALUE - MIN_VALUE) * RAND()

For example, if you want random decimal numbers between 5 and 10, you can use: **=5 + (10 - 5) * RAND()**

The result might look like this:

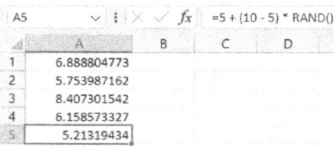

Remember, each recalculation or change in the worksheet will result in new random numbers.

RANDARRAY

The RANDARRAY formula in Excel is used to generate an **array of random numbers**. Unlike the RAND formula, RANDARRAY allows you to generate multiple random numbers at once. Here's an example of using the RANDARRAY formula:

Suppose you want to generate an array of 5 random decimal numbers in a column, say from A1 to A5. You can use the RANDARRAY formula as follows:

In cell A1, enter the formula: **=RANDARRAY(5, 1)**

This formula uses RANDARRAY to generate a column of 5 random decimal numbers. The first argument (5) specifies the number of rows, and the second argument (1) specifies the number of columns.

The result might look like this:

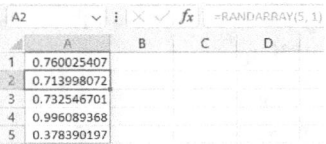

Similarly, you can use RANDARRAY to generate random decimal numbers within a specific range. For example, if you want random decimal numbers between 5 and 10: **=5 + (10 - 5) * RANDARRAY(5, 1)**

This will give you an array of 5 random decimal numbers between 5 and 10.

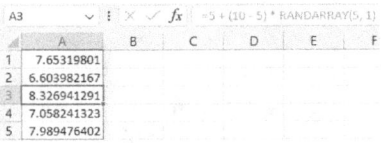

Remember, each recalculation or change in the worksheet will result in new random numbers when using RANDARRAY.

RANDBETWEEN

The RANDBETWEEN formula in Excel is used to generate a **random integer between two specified values**. Here's an example of using the RANDBETWEEN formula:

Suppose you want to generate a random integer between 1 and 100. You can use the RANDEETWEEN formula as follows:

In cell A1, enter the formula: **=RANDBETWEEN(1, 100)**

This formula uses RANDBETWEEN to generate a random integer between 1 and 100 (inclusive).

Drag the fill handle down from the bottom-right corner of cell A1 to fill the cells with random integers.

The result might look like this:

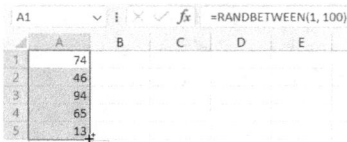

Every time you make a change to the worksheet or recalculate, Excel will generate new random integers.

If you want to generate a column of random integers within a specific range, you can adjust the formula accordingly. For example, if you want random integers between 50 and 100: **=RANDBETWEEN(50, 100)**

This will generate random integers between 50 and 100 in each cell.

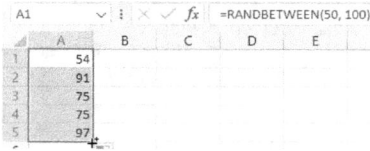

Remember that the RANDBETWEEN formula is recalculated whenever there's a change in the worksheet or when you explicitly recalculate.

RATE

The RATE formula in Excel is used to calculate the **interest rate per period for an investment based on constant payments and a constant interest rate**. Here's an example where the RATE formula is applied to calculate the interest rate for a loan.

Suppose you have the following data:

- Loan amount: $10,000 (cell A1)
- Monthly payment: -$500 (negative because it's an outgoing payment, cell B1)
- Number of payments: 36 (cell C1)

In cell D1, enter the following formula to calculate the interest rate using the RATE formula: **=RATE(C1, B1, A1)**

This formula uses the RATE formula to calculate the interest rate. Here's a breakdown of the arguments:

- **C1**: Number of periods (number of payments).
- **B1**: Payment made each period (monthly payment, with a negative sign).
- **A1**: Loan amount.

The result will be the interest rate per period. The result might look like this:

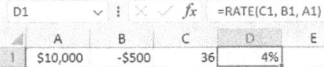

In this example, the interest rate for a $10,000 loan with a monthly payment of -$500 and a loan term of 36 months is approximately 4%.

Drag the fill handle down to extend the formula for multiple scenarios.

You can adjust the values in cells A1, B1, and C1 to model different loan scenarios and calculate the interest rate accordingly.

RIGHT

See: LEFT formula.

ROUND

The ROUND formula in Excel is used to **round a number** to a specified number of digits. Here s an example where the ROUND formula is applied to round numbers to a certain number of decimal places.

Suppose you have a list of numbers in column A, and you want to round them to two decimal places.

A1		fx	3.456	
	A	B	C	D
1	3.456			
2	8.912			
3	6.789			
4	9.123			

In this example, you can use the ROUND formula to round the numbers in column A to two decimal places.

In cell B1, enter the following formula: **=ROUND(A1, 2)**

This formula uses the ROUND formula to round the number in cell A1 to two decimal places.

Drag the fill handle down from the bottom-right corner of cell B1 to fill the cells with rounded numbers.

The result will be:

B4			fx	=ROUND(A4, 2)	
	A	B	C	D	
1	3.456	3.46			
2	8.912	8.91			
3	6.789	6.79			
4	9.123	9.12			

Now, column B contains the numbers from column A rounded to two decimal places using the ROUND formula.

You can adjust the formula based on your specific needs, such as changing the number of decimal places or rounding to a different digit.

ROUNDDOWN

The ROUNDDOWN formula in Excel is used to **round a number down** towards zero, to a specified number of digits. Here's an example where the ROUNDDOWN formula is applied to round numbers down to the nearest whole number.

Suppose you have a list of numbers in column A, and you want to round them down to the nearest whole number.

A1			fx	3.456	
	A	B	C	D	
1	3.456				
2	8.912				
3	6.789				
4	9.123				

In this example, you can use the ROUNDDOWN formula to round the numbers in column A down to the nearest whole number.

In cell B1, enter the following formula: **=ROUNDDOWN(A1, 0)**

This formula uses the ROUNDDOWN formula to round the number in cell A1 down to zero decimal places (the nearest whole number).

Drag the fill handle down from the bottom-right corner of cell B1 to fill the cells with rounded-down numbers.

The result will be:

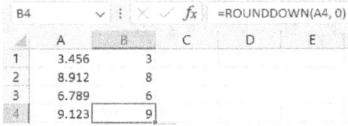

Now, column B contains the numbers from column A rounded down to the nearest whole number using the ROUNDDOWN formula.

You can adjust the formula based on your specific needs, such as rounding down to a different number of decimal places.

ROUNDUP

The ROUNDUP formula in Excel is used to round a number up, away from zero, to a specified number of digits. Here's an example where the ROUNDUP formula is applied to round numbers up to the nearest whole number.

Suppose you have a list of numbers in column A, and you want to round them up to the nearest whole number.

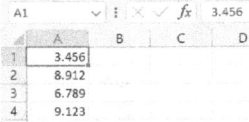

In this example, you can use the ROUNDUP formula to round the numbers in column A up to the nearest whole number.

In cell B1, enter the following formula: **=ROUNDUP(A1, 0)**

This formula uses the ROUNDUP formula to round the number in cell A1 up to zero decimal places (the nearest whole number).

Drag the fill handle down from the bottom-right corner of cell B1 to fill the cells with rounded-up numbers.

The result will be:

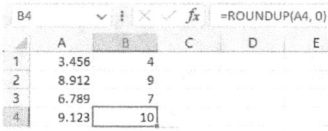

B4				fx	=ROUNDUP(A4, 0)	
	A	B	C	D	E	
1	3.456	4				
2	8.912	9				
3	6.789	7				
4	9.123	10				

Now, column B contains the numbers from column A rounded up to the nearest whole number using the ROUNDUP formula.

You can adjust the formula based on your specific needs, such as rounding up to a different number of decimal places.

SECOND

The SECOND formula in Excel is used to **extract the seconds portion of a time**. However, it's important to note that this formula is typically used with cells containing time values. If you have a cell with a time value and you want to extract the seconds from it, you can use the SECOND formula.

Here's an example:

Suppose you have a list of time values in column A:

A4				fx	10:05:37 AM
	A	B	C	D	
1	12:34:56				
2	9:45:23				
3	14:27:18				
4	10:05:37				

In this example, you can use the SECOND formula in cell B1 to extract the seconds from the time in cell A1. Enter the following formula: **=SECOND(A1)**

Drag the fill handle down from the bottom-right corner of cell B1 to fill the cells with the extracted seconds.

The result will be:

B4				fx	=SECOND(A4)
	A	B	C	D	
1	12:34:56	56			
2	9:45:23	23			
3	14:27:18	18			
4	10:05:37	37			

Now, column B contains the seconds extracted from the time values in column A using the SECOND formula.

Keep in mind that the SECOND formula extracts the seconds as integers. If you're working with date and time in a different format or you want more control over the output, you might need to use other formulas in combination, such as HOUR, MINUTE, and TEXT.

SEQUENCE

The SEQUENCE formula in Excel is used to generate a **sequence of numbers**. It's particularly useful for creating a series of sequential numbers in a row or column. Here's an example where the SEQUENCE formula is applied to generate a series of numbers.

Suppose you want to create a column of numbers from 1 to 10.

In cell A1, enter the following formula: **=SEQUENCE(10, 1, 1, 1)**

This formula uses the SEQUENCE formula to generate a column of 10 numbers starting from 1, with a step of 1.

Drag the fill handle down from the bottom-right corner of cell A1 to fill the cells with the sequence. The result will be:

Now, column A contains a sequence of numbers from 1 to 10, generated using the SEQUENCE formula.

You can customize the formula based on your needs. The arguments in the formula are as follows:

- **10**: The number of rows or columns in the sequence.
- **1**: The number of columns in the sequence.
- **1**: The starting value.
- **1**: The step value (the difference between each number in the sequence).

Adjust these arguments as necessary to create different sequences based on your requirements.

SORT

The SORT formula in Excel is used to **sort a range of cells** based on the values in one or more columns. Here's an example where the SORT formula is applied to sort a list of names alphabetically.

Suppose you have a list of names in column A:

In this example, you can use the SORT formula to sort the names alphabetically.

In cell B1, enter the following formula: **=SORT(A1:A4)**

This formula uses the SORT formula to sort the names in column A in ascending order. The result will be:

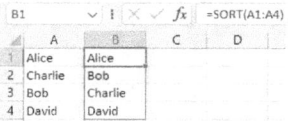

Now, column B contains the sorted names alphabetically based on the values in column A.

If you want to sort the names in descending order, you can use the following formula: **=SORT(A1:A4,,-1)**

The `-1` as the third argument indicates descending order. The result will be:

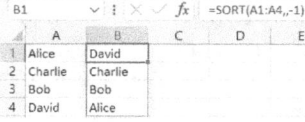

Now, column B contains the names sorted in descending order.

You can also sort based on multiple columns by providing additional column references in the SORT formula.

SQRT

The SQRT formula in Excel is used to calculate the **square root of a number**. Here's an example where the SQRT formula is applied to find the square root of numbers in a column.

Suppose you have a list of numbers in column A, and you want to find the square root of each number.

	A
1	256
2	121
3	64
4	9

In this example, you can use the SQRT formula to calculate the square root of the numbers in column A.

In cell B1, enter the following formula: **=SQRT(A1)**

This formula uses the SQRT formula to calculate the square root of the number in cell A1.

Drag the fill handle down from the bottom-right corner of cell B1 to fill the cells with square roots. The result will be:

B4		✓ ⋮ ✕ ✓	fx	=SQRT(A4)	
	A	B	C	D	
1	256	16			
2	121	11			
3	64	8			
4	9	3			

Now, column B contains the square root of the numbers in column A, calculated using the SQRT formula.

You can adjust the formula based on your specific needs or use the SQRT formula in other calculations where square roots are required.

SUBTOTAL

The SUBTOTAL formula in Excel is used to perform **calculations on a range of data**, and it is often used in conjunction with other formulas like SUM, AVERAGE, COUNT, etc. The SUBTOTAL formula allows you to perform calculations on filtered or hidden data. Here's an example where the SUBTOTAL formula is applied to calculate the sum of a range, considering only visible cells after filtering.

Suppose you have a list of numbers in column A, and you want to calculate the sum of these numbers after applying a filter.

	A
1	5
2	8
3	10
4	3

In cell B1, enter the following formula using the SUBTOTAL formula: **=SUBTOTAL(109, A:A)**

This formula uses the SUBTOTAL formula with formula number 109, which corresponds to the SUM formula, and the range A:A.

The result will be:

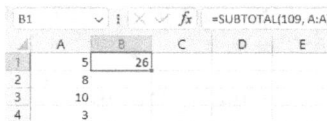

column B contains the sum of cells in column A.

1. Apply a filter to your data by selecting the column header (cell A1 in this case) and clicking on the "Filter" button in the toolbar.
2. Filter the data to include only values greater than 5.
3. Now, column B contains the sum of the visible cells in column A after filtering.

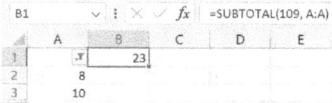

You can adjust the formula number in the SUBTOTAL formula to perform different calculations such as averages, counts, maximums, minimums, etc. The SUBTOTAL formula automatically takes into account only the visible cells based on the applied filter or hidden rows.

SUM

The SUM formula is commonly used to **add up a range of numbers** in Excel. Here's a practical example:

Let's say you have a column of numbers representing sales figures for a company in cells A1 through A5:

	A
1	100
2	150
3	200
4	120
5	180

To find the total sales, you can use the SUM formula. Here's how you would do it:

1. Select the cell where you want the total to appear. Let's say you want the total in cell B1.
2. Type the following formula: **=SUM(A1:A5)**
3. Press **Enter**.

Excel will calculate the sum of the numbers in the range A1 to A5 and display the result in the selected cell (B1 in this case). The formula **=SUM(A1:A5)** adds up all the numbers in cells A1 through A5. The result in cell B1 will be:

B1			fx	=SUM(A1:A5)
	A	B	C	D
1	100	750		
2	150			
3	200			
4	120			
5	180			

So, the practical application here is using the SUM formula to quickly calculate the total sales without manually adding each individual value. This is especially useful when dealing with large datasets where manual addition would be time-consuming and prone to errors.

SUMIF

The SUMIF formula in Excel is used to **sum values in a range based on a given condition**. Here's an example where the SUMIF formula is applied to sum values in a range that meet a specific criterion.

Suppose you have a list of sales in column A and corresponding product categories in column B. You want to calculate the total sales for a specific category, let's say "Electronics."

	A	B
1	200	Electronics
2	150	Clothing
3	300	Electronics
4	180	Furniture
5	250	Electronics

In this example, you can use the SUMIF formula to calculate the total sales for the "Electronics" category.

In cell C1, enter the following formula: **=SUMIF(B:B, "Electronics", A:A)**

This formula uses the SUMIF formula with the following arguments:

- **B:B**: The range that contains the criteria (product categories).
- **"Electronics"**: The criterion to sum values.
- **A:A**: The range to sum values from (sales).

The result will be:

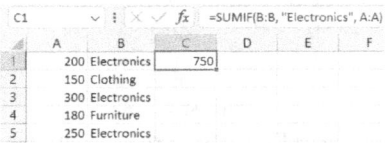

Now, column C contains the total sales for the "Electronics" category.

You can adjust the criteria and ranges in the SUMIF formula based on your specific needs. This formula is useful for summarizing data based on specific conditions.

SUMIFS

The SUMIFS formula in Excel is used to **sum values in a range based on multiple criteria**. Here's an example where the SUMIFS formula is applied to sum values in a range that meet multiple conditions.

Suppose you have a sales dataset with columns for sales amounts (column A), product categories (column B), and regions (column C). You want to calculate the total sales for the "Electronics" category in the "East" region.

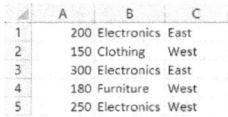

In this example, you can use the SUMIFS formula to calculate the total sales for the "Electronics" category in the "East" region.

In cell D1, enter the following formula: **=SUMIFS(A:A, B:B, "Electronics", C:C, "East")**

This formula uses the SUMIFS formula with the following arguments:

- **A:A**: The range that contains the values to sum (sales).

- **B:B**: The range that contains the first criteria (product categories).
- **"Electronics"**: The criterion to sum values based on the first criteria.
- **C:C**: The range that contains the second criteria (regions).
- **"East"**: The criterion to sum values based on the second criteria.

The result will be:

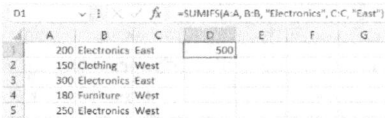

Now, column D contains the total sales for the "Electronics" category in the "East" region.

You can add more criteria to the SUMIFS formula if needed, making it a versatile tool for summing data based on multiple conditions.

SUMPRODUCT

The SUMPRODUCT formula in Excel is used to multiply corresponding elements in arrays and then **sum the products**. It's a versatile formula that can be used for various calculations. Here's an example where the SUMPRODUCT formula is applied to calculate the total sales amount by multiplying quantity and price.

Suppose you have a dataset with columns for product names (column A), quantity sold (column B), and unit price (column C).

	A	B	C
1	Product 1	10	20
2	Product 2	5	15
3	Product 3	12	25
4	Product 4	8	18

In this example, you can use the SUMPRODUCT formula to calculate the total sales amount by multiplying quantity and price for each product.

In cell D1, enter the following formula: **=SUMPRODUCT(B:B, C:C)**

This formula uses the SUMPRODUCT formula to multiply corresponding elements in the arrays B:B (quantity) and C:C (price), and then sum the products.

The result will be:

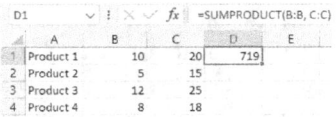

Now, column D contains the total sales amount for each product, calculated using the SUMPRODUCT formula.

You can modify the ranges in the formula based on your specific dataset and the columns containing the quantity and price values. The SUMPRODUCT formula is powerful for performing calculations that involve multiplying and summing corresponding elements in arrays.

SWITCH

The SWITCH formula in Excel is used to **evaluate a given expression against a list of values and return the result associated with the first matching value**. Here's an example where the SWITCH formula is applied to categorize products based on their sales.

Suppose you have a dataset with product names in column A and corresponding sales amounts in column B.

	A	B
1	Product 1	100
2	Product 2	250
3	Product 3	80
4	Product 4	200

Now, let's use the SWITCH formula to categorize the products based on their sales into "Low," "Medium," or "High."

In cell C1, enter the following formula:

=SWITCH(TRUE(), B1<100, "Low", B1<200, "Medium", B1>=200, "High")

This formula uses the SWITCH formula to evaluate the sales amount in cell B1 against a series of conditions:

- If the sales are less than 100, it returns "Low."
- If the sales are less than 200, it returns "Medium."
- If the sales are 200 or greater, it returns "High."

Drag the fill handle down from the bottom-right corner of cell C1 to fill the cells with the corresponding categories for each product.

The result will be:

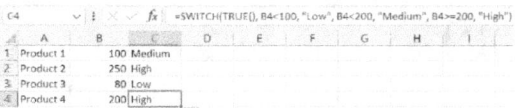

Now, column C contains the categories ("Low," "Medium," or "High") assigned to each product based on its sales amount, using the SWITCH formula.

You can customize the conditions and categories in the SWITCH formula based on your specific criteria.

TEXT

The TEXT formula in Excel is used to **format a number or date as text** using a specified format code. Here's an example where the TEXT formula is applied to format a date.

Suppose you have a date in cell C1 and you want to display it in a different format.

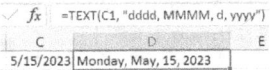

In this example, you can use the TEXT formula to format the date in cell C1.

In cell D1, enter the following formula: **=TEXT(C1, "dddd, MMMM d, yyyy")**

This formula uses the TEXT formula to format the date in cell C1 with the specified format code. The format code "dddd, MMMM d, yyyy" will display the full day name, full month name, day of the month, and the year.

The result will be:

Now, column D contains the formatted date based on the TEXT formula.

You can customize the format code in the TEXT formula to display the date in different formats according to your preferences. The TEXT formula is versatile and can be used for formatting both dates and numbers.

TEXTJOIN

The TEXTJOIN formula in Excel is used to **concatenate text from multiple ranges or values using a specified delimiter**. Here's an example where the TEXTJOIN formula is applied to concatenate names from a list.

Suppose you have a list of names in column A, and you want to concatenate these names into a single cell with a comma as the delimiter.

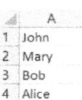

In this example, you can use the TEXTJOIN formula to concatenate the names in column A.

In cell B1, enter the following formula: **=TEXTJOIN(", ", TRUE, A1:A4)**

This formula uses the TEXTJOIN formula with the following arguments:

- **", "**: The delimiter to be used between the concatenated values (a comma and a space).
- **TRUE**: Ignoring empty cells in the range.
- **A1:A4**: The range containing the names to be concatenated.

The result will be:

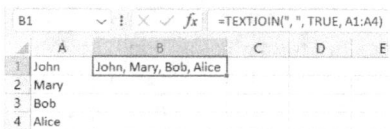

Now, cell B1 contains the concatenated names with a comma and space as the delimiter, using the TEXTJOIN formula.

You can customize the formula based on your specific needs, such as changing the delimiter or including/excluding empty cells in the concatenation. The TEXTJOIN formula is flexible and powerful for joining text from multiple cells.

TIME

The TIME formula in Excel is used to create a **time value** based on specified hours, minutes, and seconds. Here's an example where the TIME formula is applied to create a time value.

Suppose you want to create a time value representing 3 hours, 30 minutes, and 45 seconds.

In cell A1, enter the following formula: **=TIME(3, 30, 45)**

This formula uses the TIME formula with three arguments:

- **3**: The number of hours.
- **30**: The number of minutes.
- **45**: The number of seconds.

The result will be a time value representing 3 hours, 30 minutes, and 45 seconds.

Now, you can format the cell to display the time value in your preferred time format. Right-click on the cell, choose "Format Cells," and select the desired time format:

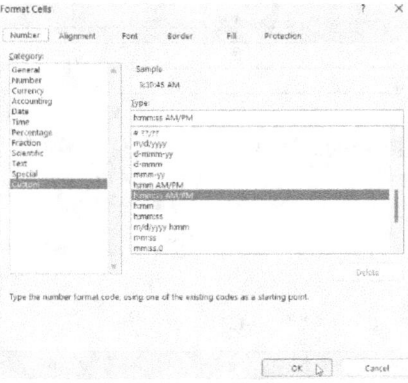

The result might look like this:

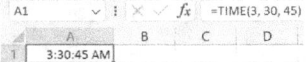

Now, cell A1 contains the time value representing 3 hours, 30 minutes, and 45 seconds, created using the TIME formula.

You can adjust the formula based on your specific time requirements by changing the values in the TIME formula's arguments. The TIME formula is useful for creating time values that can be used in calculations or displayed in a specific format.

TRANSPOSE

The TRANSPOSE formula in Excel is used to **flip or rotate the orientation of a range of cells**. It's particularly useful when you want to switch rows to columns or vice versa. Here's an example where the TRANSPOSE formula is applied to transpose a range of data.

Suppose you have a dataset in columns A and B:

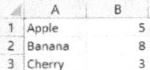

In this example, you can use the TRANSPOSE formula to switch the rows and columns.

1. Select the destination range where you want to transpose the data. For example, select cells **D1:F2**.

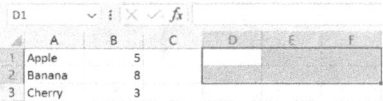

2. Enter the following formula: **=TRANSPOSE(A1:B3)**

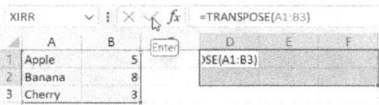

3. Press Enter, press **Ctrl+Shift+Enter**.

The result will be:

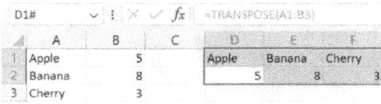

Now, cells D1:F2 contain the transposed data, with rows becoming columns and columns becoming rows.

Keep in mind that the destination range must have enough cells to accommodate the transposed data. Also, any changes in the original data will be reflected in the transposed data, as they are linked.

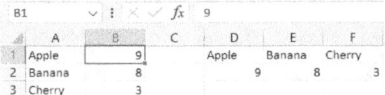

This example demonstrates the basic use of the TRANSPOSE formula for switching rows and columns.

TRIM

The TRIM formula in Excel is used to **remove leading and trailing spaces from a text string** and also to **reduce multiple consecutive spaces between words to a single space**. Here's an example where the TRIM formula is applied to clean up text.

Suppose you have a dataset in column A with names that include unnecessary leading and trailing spaces:

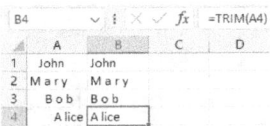

In this example, you can use the TRIM formula to remove the leading, and trailing spaces from the names in column A.

In cell B1, enter the following formula: =TRIM(A1)

Drag the fill handle down from the bottom-right corner of cell B1 to fill the cells with the TRIM formula.

The result will be:

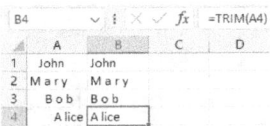

Now, column B contains the names without leading and trailing spaces, cleaned up using the TRIM formula.

You can apply the TRIM formula to clean up text strings in various scenarios, such as when dealing with data imported from external sources or when users may inadvertently include extra spaces in input.

UNIQUE

The **UNIQUE** formula in Excel is used to **extract unique values** from a range or array. Here's an example to demonstrate how it works:

Suppose you have a list of names in column A, and you want to extract the unique names.

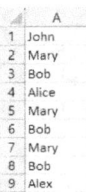

In column B, you can use the UNIQUE formula to achieve this. Assuming your data starts from cell A1, you would enter the following formula in cell B1:

=UNIQUE(A1:A9)

This formula will extract unique values from the range A1 to A9 and display them in column B. Adjust the range as needed based on your actual data.

Example:

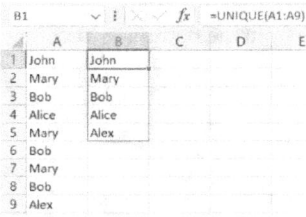

In this example, the **UNIQUE** formula in cell B1 extracts unique names from column A, and the result is displayed in column B. As you can see, duplicate names are removed, and only the unique names are listed.

UPPER

The UPPER formula in Excel is used to **convert text to uppercase**. Here's an example to demonstrate how it works:

Let's say you have a list of names in column A, and you want to convert all of them to uppercase in column B.

Assuming your data starts from cell A1, you would enter the following formula in cell B1: **=UPPER(A1)**

This formula will convert the text in cell A1 to uppercase. You can then drag this formula down to apply it to the entire column. Example:

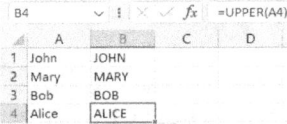

In this example, the `UPPER` formula is applied to each name in column A, converting them all to uppercase. Adjust the range as needed based on your actual data.

Keep in mind that the `UPPER` formula does not modify the original text; it only returns the uppercase version. If you want to permanently convert the text to uppercase, you can copy the results in column B and use "Paste Values" to overwrite the original values.

VLOOKUP

The VLOOKUP formula in Excel is used to **search for a value in the first column of a table and return a value in the same row from another column**. Here's an example to demonstrate how it works:

Let's say you have a table that contains employee information with employee IDs in column A, names in column B, and salaries in column C.

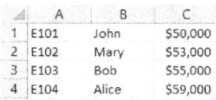

You want to find the salary of a specific employee based on their ID. Assuming your data starts from cell A1, and you want to find the salary for the employee with ID "E103," you would use the following formula:

=VLOOKUP("E103", A1:C4, 3, FALSE)

This formula looks for the value "E103" in the first column (A1:A10) of the table, and if it finds a match, it returns the corresponding value from the third column (C1:C4), which represents the salary. The "FALSE" parameter indicates that an exact match is required.

Example:

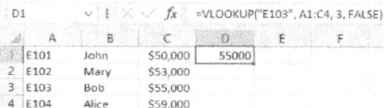

In this example, the `VLOOKUP` formula is used to find the salary for the employee with ID "E103," and it returns the result as "55000." Adjust the range and search value based on your actual data.

WEEKDAY

The WEEKDAY formula in Excel is used to return the **day of the week for a given date**. Here's an example to demonstrate how it works:

Suppose you have a list of dates in column A.

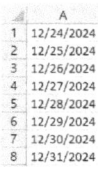

You want to find the corresponding day of the week in column B. Assuming your dates start from cell A1, you would enter the following formula in cell B1:
=WEEKDAY(A1)

This formula will return a number representing the day of the week, where Sunday is 1 and Saturday is 7.

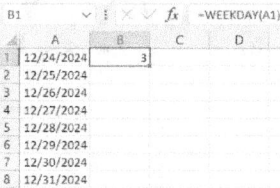

If you want the result to be the actual name of the day, you can use the `TEXT` formula as well. For example: **=TEXT(A1, "dddd")**

This formula will return the full name of the day.

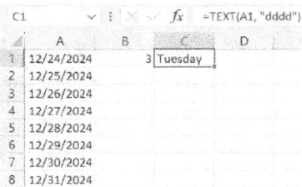

Example:

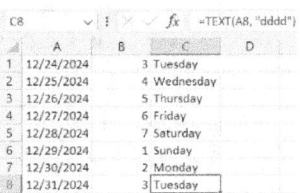

In this example, the WEEKDAY formula is used to find the day of the week for each date in column A, and the results are displayed in column B. Adjust the range and formatting options based on your actual data.

WORKDAY

The WORKDAY formula in Excel is used to calculate a date that is a specified **number of working days** (excluding weekends and optionally, specified holidays) ahead of or behind a given date. Here's an example to demonstrate how it works:

Suppose you have a start date in cell A1, and you want to find the date that is 5 working days ahead, excluding weekends (Saturday and Sunday). You would use the following formula in cell B1: **=WORKDAY(A1, 5)**

This formula calculates a date that is 5 working days (excluding weekends) ahead of the date in cell A1.

Example:

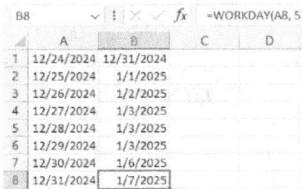

In this example, the `WORKDAY` formula is used to calculate the date that is 5 working days ahead of the dates in column A, and the results are displayed in column B.

XLOOKUP

The XLOOKUP formula in Excel is a powerful lookup and reference formula. It can be used to **search a range or array, find the first match, and return the corresponding value**. Here's an example:

Suppose you have a list of products in column A, and their corresponding prices in column B. You want to find the price of a specific product.

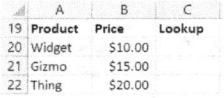

Assuming your data starts from cell A2, and you want to find the price of "Gizmo" in cell C3, you would use the following `XLOOKUP` formula:

=XLOOKUP("Gizmo", A2:A4, B2:B4, "Not Found")

This formula searches for the value in cell C3 ("Gizmo") in the range A2:A4, and if it finds a match, it returns the corresponding value from column B (the price). If no match is found, it returns "Not Found."

Example:

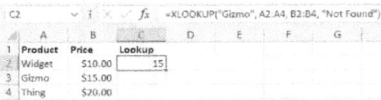

In this example, the `XLOOKUP` formula is used to find the price of the product specified in cell C3. Adjust the range and lookup value based on your actual data.

Note: `XLOOKUP` is available in Excel 365, Excel 2019, and Excel 2016 with the latest updates. If you're using an older version of Excel, you might need to use alternative lookup formulas like `VLOOKUP` or `INDEX/MATCH`.

XMATCH

The XMATCH formula in Excel is used to **search for a specified value in a range and return its relative position**. Here's an example to demonstrate how it works:

Suppose you have a list of product names in column A, and you want to find the position of a specific product in the list. Assuming your data starts from cell A2, and you want to find the position of "Gizmo" in cell A3, you would use the following `XMATCH` formula: **=XMATCH("Gizmo", A2:A10, 0)**

This formula searches for the value "Gizmo" in the range A2:A10 and returns its relative position. The "0" as the third argument indicates an exact match.

Example:

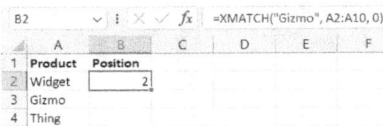

In this example, the `XMATCH` formula is used to find the position of "Gizmo" in the list of products. The result is 2 because "Gizmo" is the second item in the range A2:A10. Adjust the range and lookup value based on your actual data.

Note: `XMATCH` is available in Excel 365, Excel 2019, and Excel 2016 with the latest updates. If you're using an older version of Excel, you might need to use alternative lookup formulas like `MATCH`.

YEAR

The YEAR formula in Excel is used to **extract the year from a date**. Here's an example to demonstrate how it works:

Suppose you have a list of dates in column A, and you want to extract the year for each date in column B. Assuming your dates start from cell A1, you would enter the following `YEAR` formula in cell B1: **=YEAR(A1)**

This formula will extract the year from the date in cell A1. You can then copy this formula down to apply it to the entire column.

Example:

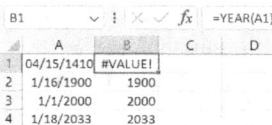

In this example, the `YEAR` formula is used to extract the year for each date in column A, and the results are displayed in column B. Adjust the range based on your actual data.

You can also use the `YEAR` formula in combination with other formulas for more advanced date manipulations, such as calculating the difference between years or performing conditional operations based on the year.

Excel does not support dates before January 1, 1900. In Excel, dates are stored as serial numbers, where January 1, 1900, is represented as 1. Dates before January 1, 1900, are not recognized by Excel.

INDEX

Cover: https://pixabay.com/vectors/excel-icon-microsoft-5963669/